2-25-74

To Judy Souceda —

With best wishes,

Neil C. Sandberg

Ethnic Identity and Assimilation: The Polish-American Community

Neil C. Sandberg
foreword by
Herbert Gans

Winner of the Kosciuszko Foundation
Dissertation Award for 1972

The Praeger Special Studies program—utilizing the most modern and efficient book production techniques and a selective worldwide distribution network—makes available to the academic, government, and business communities significant, timely research in U.S. and international economic, social, and political development.

Ethnic Identity and Assimilation: The Polish-American Community

Case Study of Metropolitan Los Angeles

PRAEGER SPECIAL STUDIES IN U.S. ECONOMIC, SOCIAL, AND POLITICAL ISSUES

Praeger Publishers   New York   Washington   London

Library of Congress Cataloging in Publication Data

Sandberg, Neil C
    Ethnic identity and assimilation.

    (Praeger special studies in U.S. economic, social,
and political issues)
    Includes bibliographical references.
    1. Poles in Los Angeles.   I.   Title.
F869. L89P77   301. 45'19'185079494   73-10955

PRAEGER PUBLISHERS
111 Fourth Avenue, New York, N.Y. 10003, U.S.A.
5, Cromwell Place, London SW7, 2JL, England

Published in the United States of America in 1974
by Praeger Publishers, Inc.

Printed in the United States of America

ACKNOWLEDGMENTS

I am grateful to Herbert Gans for accepting my invitation to write the foreword to this book. His thoughtful analysis of ethnicity is generally consistent with the data generated by this study.

As the reader will note, I hold the view that the future of ethnicity is threatened but has yet to be decided. Hence, I am between those who predict its continued decline and others who anticipate its resurgence.

A number of individuals assisted me in this study. Professor Lyle Knowles, chairman of my doctoral dissertation committee, contributed greatly to the development of the group cohesiveness scale through his knowledge of research methods. His teaching skills and his insights and personal encouragement were invaluable throughout the entire project.

Judith Herman, Irving Levine, and Murray Friedman of the American Jewish Committee staff added substantially to my understanding of the ethnic dimension in American life. The support of the AJC was also very helpful.

The cooperation of Mrs. Antoinette Rydzeski was most important; indeed, the study would have been enormously difficult without her efforts. I also thank Father Jacek Przygoda for the use of his library and Mrs. Lois Marquez for her skill in preparing the manuscript.

In addition, I am indebted to Father Donald Merrifield, S.J., President of Loyola University; Sister Raymond McKay, former President of Marymount College; and Sister Helen Kelly, President of Immaculate Heart College, for facilitating interviews with a number of their students.

The major contributors to this work, however, are my wife, Mary, and my son, Curt. Their patience, understanding, and assistance made it possible for me to concentrate on the study in a trying period. This book is dedicated to them with love.

In the mid-1950s, a number of observers of American life, basing their conclusions largely on the hectic construction of churches and synagogues in the new suburbia, concluded that the country was undergoing a religious revival. A few years later, however, as more reliable data showed that church and synagogue attendance continued to decline, the alleged religious revival was quietly forgotten.

I am reminded of this bit of history because there is currently much talk about another revival—the revival of ethnic pride and identity. A number of intellectuals, particularly from Irish, Italian, Slovak, and Polish groups, are arguing that these "ethnics" are developing a new interest in their ethnic identity and are even reviving the long-dormant ethnic cultures. Once again, there is some evidence to support the claim of revival—the increased ethnic symbolism in various recent local and national elections—but once again, I don't think this limited datum supports the larger generalization, and I suspect that in a few years the revival of ethnicity will also be forgotten.

This is one conclusion I draw from Neil Sandberg's study of ethnic attitudes among a sample of Polish-Americans in California. Dr. Sandberg shows that while his respondents continue to express attitudes in support of many facets of Polish identity and culture, these attitudes decline in number and intensity both with later generational origin and higher social class, although not in a perfectly linear pattern. Thus, if Sandberg's data apply to other Polish-Americans, as I suspect they do, by the time the majority of Polish-Americans are fourth generation and middle class, their identification with Polish-American culture and society is likely to be quite weak, and their participation in them even more so. Attitude studies probably overstate interest in ethnicity, if only because it is easier for a respondent to say that he or she favors participating in Polish life than to actually do so. Consequently, it is quite possible that the extent of ethnic participation among Dr. Sandberg's respondents is less than what is expressed in their attitudes. Dr. Sandberg's study came up with many other interesting findings, but since his book is short, I shall refrain from the usual foreword writer's practice of summarizing the findings, and will instead discuss what I consider to be the current state of ethnicity in America.

Ever since the 1950s when I became involved in ethnic research, first among suburban Jews and then among urban Italian-Americans, I have been

---
Herbert J. Gans is Professor of Sociology, Columbia University and Senior Research Associate, Center for Policy Research.

convinced that ethnicity in America is best understood by what Sandberg calls the "straight line theory." This theory, already suggested by W. Lloyd Warner and Leo Srole in their mid-1930s study of ethnic groups in "Yankee City," argues that the life of American ethnic groups, particularly Catholic ones of peasant origin such as Polish-Americans, is marked by a continuing process of acculturation and assimilation that is not likely to be reversed in the future. Acculturation is concerned with the giving up of the ethnic culture in favor of main-stream American culture. It has proceeded at such a rapid pace that the majority of ethnics have already adopted American ways of life by the second generation (the first native-born generation), relegating ethnic customs, arts, dances, and music to ceremonial occasions, and even giving up many ethnic food habits and religious practices. Assimilation, which refers to social and other relationships with people of non-ethnic background, has also proceeded, but far more slowly, and many ethnics still socialize with and marry people of the same national origin, and live in urban neighborhoods and suburban subdivisions in which a plurality of the residents are from the same ethnic group.

Unfortunately, there has been little sociological research among ethnic groups lately, and almost nothing is known about the third generation, which will soon be the majority among most of the ethnic groups whose ancestors came from Central and Eastern Europe. In fact, Sandberg's study is one of the few that provides data on them and on the so far unstudied fourth generation. I suspect, however, that assimilation is escalating among these generations and that fewer and fewer people find it necessary or desirable to select their neighbors, friends, and spouses from their own ethnic groups. There are some data that point to a good deal of intermarriage, at least between ethnic groups who are Catholic, and also between Jews and non-Jews, at least in the smaller cities and towns where Jewish spouses are hard to find. Intermarriage between Catholic ethnics is not new, and already during the 1950s, Will Herberg, drawing on the sociological research of Ruby Jo Kennedy, argued that ethnic identity would eventually be replaced by religious identity and that Americans would then identify themselves with one of three major religions, Catholicism, Protestantism, and Judaism. This has not happened, however, and for three reasons. First, religious observance has become less important to people in the last two decades, and some recent polls suggest that even Catholics, who previously came faithfully to Mass every week, are now coming less often. In the long run, it is quite possible that all American religions are going to be twice-a-year institutions, with most Christians attending church only at Easter and Christmas, and most Jews going to synagogue only at Rosh Hashana and Yom Kippur. Second, the taboo on religious intermarriage, still strong in the 1950s, has weakened considerably, particularly among Jews; and third, religious denominationalism still plays an important social role. For example, as long as Episcopalianism is identified with the upper class and Pentecostal Baptism with the lower class, it is hard to imagine that rich and poor Protestants would be willing to accept the same non-denominational religious label.

The holding power of ethnicity is weaker than that of religion, and reasons for the steady progress of acculturation and assimilation are not hard to find. The Catholic ethnics who came to America were largely peasants or farm laborers, who in their homelands were so poor and deprived that they had neither the opportunity nor the right to share in the national cultures that were created mainly by and for intellectuals and aristocrats. Indeed, they developed their own peasant cultures. Moreover they had little reason to identify with their homelands, in part because these treated them badly, in part because as peasants, they lived in towns or villages that had little contact with the nation of which they were officially a part. In fact, as Nathan Glazer has pointed out, only after coming to America have peasant ethnics realized that they were Poles or Italians.

In America, most of the peasants became an urban proletariat, and almost at once had to shed those parts of their peasant culture which conflicted with their need to survive in the cities. Thus, little of it was passed on to the native-born second generation, which in turn jettisoned much of the rest for lack of relevance. Moreover as that generation began to strive for mobility, it found ethnic culture, like much of the rest of its ethnic heritage, a hindrance and it has so remained for later generations despite the greater tolerance for ethnicity that has developed in recent years. Peasant culture is fatalistic and thus exactly the reverse of what is needed by mobile people. But even those few third- and fourth-generation ethnics who have achieved sufficient mobility and may recently have become curious about their ethnic origins are not likely to reverse the acculturative trend. For one thing, by now they are Americans who live in an American culture that they find relevant and satisfying—in part because it is much less WASPish than the American culture their ancestors confronted when they came off the boat. In addition, the ancestral ethnic culture of their homelands no longer exists, as ethnic Americans who have visited their ancestral lands have discovered. In most of these countries, even in Eastern Europe, a modern, non-aristocratic and non-intellectual culture is now developing. The new culture is itself borrowing from America as much and as quickly as it can, and is therefore not of great interest to American ethnics nostalgic for their ancestral culture. As a result, even the raw materials for an ethnic cultural revival in America are unavailable, and despite the claim of some ethnic intellectuals, so is the interest for such a revival.

Assimilation has proceeded more slowly than acculturation because people change their social structures and relationships more slowly than their cultures or attitudes. Birds of a feather flock together, and the more so when they are discriminated against or thought to be of low status, as was the case for the Catholic ethnic groups in America until the last decade or so. As these ethnics achieve middle-class status and discrimination disappears, and as they shed the occupations traditionally associated with their ethnic group, they are able to make contact with other Americans. As they find that their basic values and attitudes are not very different, the incentives for assimilation increase. Now assimilation is no longer the name-changing and rejection of origins necessary for mobility that was associated with the first and second generation, but it becomes a spontaneous and almost unconscious process of discovering that the people one finds compatible as neighbors, friends, and spouses do not necessarily have to come from one's own ethnic group. For example, fourth-generation Polish-Americans may find that the fourth-generation Italian-Americans they meet at college are socially, culturally, and emotionally much like themselves, and the national origin of their respective great-grandparents is irrelevant. This is true, however, only if they are similar in socio-economic level, but when they are, a lower-middle-class Polish-American may well have more in common with a lower-middle-class Italian-American than with a upper-middle-class member of his own ethnic group.

The likelihood of a reversal of assimilatory trends is also small because there is nothing in American society that would encourage or require Polish-Americans, or members of any other ethnic group, to interact on the basis of common ethnicity. The individual ethnic groups no longer monopolize any one occupation or industry, and conversely, no ethnic group is concentrated in one occupation and industry, so that it is hard to imagine that any ethnic group would coalesce for economic reasons. A recurrence of intense and widespread anti-semitism would undoubtedly reverse assimilatory trends among Jews, but the Catholic ethnic groups have never suffered from the same kind of discrimination as the Jews and are not likely to so suffer in the future. They were discriminated against for being European peasants and of low status but they are today neither, and judging from Sandberg's data, the third- and fourth-generation Polish-Americans he studied did not even seem to be excessively bothered by the mass media's telling of the highly insulting Polish jokes.

The continuation of acculturation and assimilation does not mean that all remnants of ethnicity have disappeared or will disappear shortly. The remains of old ethnic cultures will continue to be maintained in museums and scholarly writings and will be practiced at religious and secular festivals, if only once or twice a year. Ethnicity is also still a social cement, even if of less and continually decreasing strength. However, many Catholic ethnics are still part of the working class, either by occupation or by way of life, and thus continue to emphasize the family circle in which relatives are also friends so that their social life is still dominated by members of their own ethnic group. By and large, American ethnicity today is working-class ethnicity, and the congruence between being working class and feeling ethnic is well brought out by Dr. Sandberg's study. Most important, ethnic identification continues to persist, and people still think of themselves as Polish-Americans, even in California, which is conventionally thought to be much less concerned with ethnicity than the Northeast or Midwest. Ethnic identification also persists among third- and fourth-generation ethnics, as Dr. Sandberg demonstrates, but as his Table 5.20 suggests, it is not very strong, and it seems clear that ethnicity does not play a significant role in their lives. And as more Polish-Americans and other ethnics become more middle class and American in the third and fourth generations, ethnicity will be less and less important to them.

Consequently, it becomes relevant to ask why there is currently so much talk of an ethnic revival in America. To some extent that talk is a wishful extension of the nostalgia for simpler times that is gripping many Americans as their contemporary society becomes more conflict-ridden. It is no accident, therefore, that ethnicity is conceived to be a gut-feeling that provides some certainty in uncertain times. However, there is also some evidence of two kinds of actual revivals, one political, the other intellectual, that have been falsely wished into a wholesale ethnic cultural and social revival and a reversal of acculturation and assimilation.

The political revival has taken the form of increased ethnic political organization and especially ethnic symbolism in recent elections. There are several reasons for its occurrence. One reason is the decline of Irish and WASP control of American politics, and the political mobility of Italian-Americans, Polish-Americans, and others into important local and national positions. This political mobility has been developing for a long time and has more to do with the fact that many members of these ethnic groups have achieved middle class status, and thus economic power and political power, than with a new ethnic consciousness. Thus, America's incumbent Vice President is a Greek-American, but it would be incorrect to ascribe this to an increase in Greek identity, particularly since Mr. Agnew was not elected by the Greek community, and had in any case changed both his ancestral name and religion before he became a politician.

Second, and far more important, the urban and suburban white working class has also achieved more political power in the last few years, and since many of the members of that class are Catholic ethnics, their new influence has been falsely ascribed to a newly emerging ethnic pride. What has actually happened is that for the first time in a long time, the white working class has become politically visible, but their demands have been labeled as ethnic rather than working class. For one thing, America has always eschewed overt class politics and the use of class terminology in politics, as long as other terminologies were available. Moreover, given the taboo on class terminology and the pejorative connotation of "working class" in a predominantly middle-class society, the white working class would hardly want to describe itself or to be described as working class if ethnicity is available as a convenient substitute. Also, although the labor movement has served as the major representative and exponent of working-class demands in America, it cannot serve as a representative for people outside the unions, such as garage owners and other small working-class businessmen, or for non-work issues such as the complaints of homeowners and local taxpayers. Finally, ethnicity and ethnic pride can serve as convenient, not necessarily conscious code-words for anti-black feelings, although ethnics may also favor anti-black policies because they have ethnic needs and demands rather than because they are opposed to policies that aid blacks.

Even so, a closer look at today's so-called ethnic politics suggests that it is much less ethnic than it appears to be. It is in fact "pan-ethnic," a coalition of whites of similar socio-economic condition, age, homeownership status, and religion, who happen also to be ethnics, but their politics neither stresses ethnicity nor has anything to do with individual ethnic groups. The best example of political pan-ethnicity took place in Cleveland some years ago when its many ethnic groups coalesced under the label of "cosmopolitan" or "cosmos" to field a white mayoral candidate against black Carl Stokes. Similarly, when Mario Proccaccino ran for mayor of New York in 1969, he did not run as an Italian but as a "candidate of the little people" (read working class and lower middle class) against the "limousine liberals" (read upper middle class). And Vice President Agnew has never described himself as a spokesmen for Greeks but for all Americans who for one reason or another disliked affluent college students and upper middle class professionals of a liberal and radical bent. Also, many working class ethnics had no difficulty in voting for WASPS like Richard Nixon and George Wallace whose campaigns have always emphasized the traditional, working-class distrust of the educated and liberal upper-middle-class professional. To be sure, many Polish-Americans still prefer to vote for a Polish-American, but only if they agree with his political orientation, and as Mark Levy and Michael Kramer have pointed out, many Poles disagreed with Senator Muskie during the 1972 Presidential primaries. Sandberg's data also show that few members of his sample "would vote for a Polish political candidate rather than any other nationality regardless of political party," and this disinclination is almost as strong among first- and second-generation Polish-Americans as among later generations, and among working-class people as among middle- and upper-class ones.

The second ethnic revival is intellectual, and most of the scholarly and rhetorical discussions of the new ethnicity have come from intellectuals of Catholic ethnic origin. Undoubtedly, they feel stirrings of ethnic identity and pride, but they may be speaking more for themselves than for all or even many members of their ethnic group. Why they should express these feelings may have something to do with the fact that they are the first ethnic intellectuals and academics, at least from the Catholic ethnic groups, since the foreign-born intellectuals who came as immigrants. Until recently, many Catholic ethnics were unable or unwilling to send their children to college and those who did go, went mostly into business and engineering schools which could promise them well-paying and secure careers. In recent years, however, Catholic ethnics have finally begun to go into English, the humanities, sociology, and the other social sciences, a few have now become faculty members, and some have begun to publish. They are still a small academic minority, however, and like most minorities, they are sometimes met with overt or covert discrimination. But even when they have escaped that discrimination, they are still working amidst a predominatly WASP and Jewish set of colleagues and in an academic and intellectual world dominated by assimilationist, agnostic, and even anti-ethnic Establishments. As the pioneer ethnic intellectuals, they have emphasized both their ethnicity and their religiosity to distinguish themselves from their colleagues and defend themselves against the Establishments of their respective academic and intellectual specialities.

I must stress that I am not suggesting that they have consciously emphasized their ethnicity because they do not fit into the contemporary academic and intellectual Establishments. What has happened, rather, is that they have come into academia and the intellectual world from an ethnic milieu, and finding that their perspectives and points of view have not been considered, they have filled a vacuum that should have been filled long ago. As such, they are playing a useful role in American intellectual life, and they are wrong only when they claim to represent others than themselves, and proclaim a large-scale ethnic revival that does not actually exist. Even so, their writings are not entirely about ethnicity, and some have in fact filled another vacuum— politically conservative thought—although they have clothed it in ethnic trappings.

The intellectual revival is likely to continue as more ethnics occupy academic, literary, and other intellectual positions, although it is safe to say that eventually they too will acculturate, just as academics and intellectuals of Jewish origin have acculturated and become members of academic and intellectual Establishments. Meanwhile, it may be that the ethnic intellectual revival is a new illustration of Hansen's "Law of the Return of the Third Generation." Hansen, a Swedish-American writer, suggested that once ethnics had overcome the discrimination and marginality that he thought dominated the life of the second generation, the third generation could return to its ethnic heritage. Since Hansen's major empirical justification of his "law" came from the founding of some Swedish historical associations among third-generation Midwestern Swedish-Americans, it may be that then, as now, Hansen's Law applies only to academics and intellectuals. Certainly, Dr. Sandberg's study does not provide any evidence that the rest of the third generation is more interested in its ethnic origins than the first or second; as it makes abundantly clear, that generation continues along the paths of acculturation and assimilation which their ancestors entered the moment they came to America.

CONTENTS

LIST OF TABLES AND FIGURE

Ethnic Identity and Assimilation: The Polish-American Community

1

ETHNICITY IN AMERICA

Ethnicity has become a subject of increasing attention in American society, as social scientists, educators, and individuals from diverse groups have expressed more and more criticism of the "melting pot" theory. It had been predicted that the people from differing backgrounds would blend together into a homogeneous American prototype. But, while substantial biological and cultural assimilation did take place, there continued to be an "ethnic holding power" among many national groupings because of the common history, experience, and interests of their members.*

There are millions of ethnic Americans today, including an estimated 40 million immigrants and descendants of immigrants from eastern, southern, and central Europe. In assessing the current situation of these people, Nathan Glazer and Daniel Patrick Moynihan (1970), Hugh Davis Graham and Ted Robert Gurr (1969), and others pointed to the vitality and future potential of many of these subcommunities and disagreed with those who saw the demise of ethnic pluralism. They felt that even after their native languages and customs were lost the groups were continually re-created by new experiences, while common interests held them together in competition with other groups for the resources of society.

---

*"Ethnicity" refers to the cultural ethos of a group, its values, expectations, behavior, and the cultural characteristics that distinguish it (Marden and Meyer, 1968). "Ethnic groups" keep cultural traditions alive, help to organize the social structure, provide their members with preferred associates and opportunities for mobility and success, and enable them to identify themselves within a large and impersonal society (Greeley, 1969).

1

Some trends of the present may de-emphasize ethnic diversity, but the reality of the American past and persisting cultural variations suggests that ethnic pluralism is not just romanticism but a force in American society which has long had a role in shaping intergroup relations, and which we may be just beginning to understand (Abramson, 1970, p. 12).

Although social movements have been emphasizing group identity and interests, many individuals are searching for a new sense of self-concept, which is reflected in the reassertion of ethnic consciousness.* Andrew M. Greeley (1969), Murray Friedman (1971), and others have suggested that group identification, values, and life styles are reemerging with new vigor in spite of the general emphasis on our common American nationality. Graham and Gurr (1969) commented that this new interest in "peoplehood" has developed most particularly among young people seeking new insights into their heritage and a more meaningful sense of their place in a complex, diverse, and often impersonal society.

The heightened self-awareness among white ethnic Americans has led toward the development of new forms of communal organization and expression. This has been particularly evident as conflicts and misunderstandings fostered intergroup tensions and hostilities. The ethnics have added to the chorus of protest in America because they believe they are the forgotten Americans, not wealthy enough to derive the satisfactions of middle class life and not poor enough to benefit from public support.† Caught between the demands of blacks, Chicanos, and others on the one hand and the resistant white Anglo-Saxon Protestant (WASP) power structure on the other, large numbers of angry ethnics have been making use of political protests and group pressure in their demands to be heard (Schneider, 1970; Schroeder, 1971; and others).

The burgeoning antagonism of these groups toward other groups and toward the institutions of society has led social scientists to develop a substantial interest in ethnicity. It is hoped that an understanding of ethnic values, loyalties, and frustrations in American life will lead to prescriptions for relaxing intergroup tensions and anxieties. Moreover, it is felt that in order to ameliorate their problems white ethnics will have to learn to work toward common goals with nonwhites and others and to find more meaningful ways to articulate their demands (Krickus, 1971; Levine and Herman, 1971; and others).

---

*"Group identity" refers to that which individuals share with the others in a group, including their ethnic background, religion, history, life style, and value system (Isaacs, 1968).

†An "ethnic" is an individual who considers himself, or is considered by others, to be a member of a group with a foreign culture, or one who participates in the activities of such a group (Warner and Srole, 1945).

One of the largest immigrations to America was that from Poland, with an estimated total of 6 million foreign-born and their descendants now living in the United States. While most of the immigrants and their children settled into the ethnic enclaves of eastern and midwestern cities, increasing numbers, particularly those of the third and fourth generations, have been moving into the diverse areas of suburbia.

Some adventurous persons moved to the West, and as early as the turn of the century a dispersed and highly mobile Polish-American population was evident in the Los Angeles area. These settlers and the others who followed did not re-create the ethnic neighborhoods of the East, but adopted residential patterns that represented a prototype of the later suburban developments in which in-group associations had to be maintained across large distances and through new structures and means of communication. The adaptation processes of the Polish-Americans of Los Angeles, therefore, may offer some insights into what is now happening elsewhere as ethnic enclaves give way to the geographical and social fluidity of modern technological society.

THE THEORY

An evaluation of the current status and future potential of the Polish-Americans in Los Angeles requires some understanding of the factors that have affected their adjustment. Because American society places a premium on conformity and mobility, assimilationist pressures have been very strong, and the maintenance of individual and group identity has become increasingly difficult.

Three broad concepts of assimilation and acculturation have emerged in this century, and new theories are currently being advanced. The "melting pot" theory suggested the desirability and inevitability of biological and cultural amalgamation (Zangwill, 1909). Separation and segregation have been advocated by blacks, American Indians, and others as ways of strengthening group life, bolstering individual identity and psychological wholeness, and furthering group interests in a competitive multicultural society (Browne and Rustin, 1968; Carmichael and Hamilton, 1967; Steiner, 1968). "Cultural pluralism" was described as a process of living in both worlds at the same time in order to take advantage of primary group associations for personal, familial, and cultural needs, while utilizing secondary group contacts in the civic, economic, and political environments (Kallen, 1924).

Cultural pluralism may also distinguish between the continuity of structured in-group relationships and institutions and the disappearance of distinct cultural traits (Gordon, 1964). This notion of "structural pluralism" was particularly descriptive of Los Angeles, where ethnic groups have been less confined to the enclaves and have found new ways to maintain structured kinships despite the absence of geographical proximity. Basic to this view was the theoretical approach of Amitai Etzioni (1959), who anticipated the long-term continuity of the ethnic group as it is redefined in the suburban environment.

Assimilation and acculturation have also been the subject of differing theories about the predicted decline or resurgence of ethnicity. "Hansen's Law" pointed to an anticipated decline of ethnicity in the second generation and a resurgence in the third, with the group gradually thinning out in the fourth and succeeding generations (Hansen, 1952). Will Herberg (1960) suggested that ethnic differences tend to disappear in the third generation in the "triple melting pot," resulting in religiously identified Catholics, Protestants, and Jews who have lost their national identifications.

In his assessment of American Jewry, however, Herbert Gans (1956) saw a more or less straight line of cultural and social assimilation, with ethnic consciousness diminishing in each succeeding generation. This provided the basis for one of the hypotheses of this study, that ethnicity tends to decline generationally.

Gans (1962), R. Rennig et al. (1957), and others identified another aspect of this situation by pointing out the relatedness of ethnic values and social class factors. Milton M. Gordon (1964) amplified this by suggesting that people of the same social class tend to act alike and have the same social values, adding that they often confine their primary group social participation to the "ethclass," the social class segment within their own ethnic group.

Gordon and Gans both hypothesized that people of the same social class tend to think and behave similarly even when they have different ethnic backgrounds. Consequently, social class groupings may also become interethnic, especially where opportunities for in-group association are more limited, as in suburbia or the sprawling neighborhoods of Los Angeles.

This raised the possibility that the emergence of an increasingly affluent society with greater social and geographical mobility might contribute to the decline of ethnicity by facilitating intergroup involvement. Hence it was also important to examine the hypothesis that the salience of ethnicity is inversely related to social class.

THE PURPOSE OF THIS STUDY

The major research question of this study is as follows: What is the relationship between different generational and social class groups within the Polish-American community and the salience of ethnicity in each group?

A review of the previous research on ethnicity revealed a substantial body of literature that offered important conceptualizations and useful insights into the various aspects of ethnic identification. Their conclusions, however, were rarely based on empirical investigation.

There is very little in the literature about ethnic group cohesiveness, and there is a need for a meaningful scale for measuring ethnic commitment.* Despite interest manifested in the predicted decline of ethnicity or its resurgence, relatively few studies have been developed. Further, there have been only a limited number of investigations into such areas as social class, generational differences, and the impact of social mobility on the future of ethnicity.

This was even more evident with respect to the literature on Polonia, much of which was found to be out-dated and of limited value for social science research. (A definition of "Polonia" is to be found in the third section of Chapter 2.) Assessments of the Polish-American experience were primarily self-serving historical accounts, apparently intended to present a favorable image of the group to America. Although substantial efforts have been made by a number of Polish scholars the output has been relatively narrow, especially in the realm of sociological and psychological research.

Consequently, since it was extremely difficult to develop meaningful comparative studies, it was necessary to create a group cohesiveness scale to measure ethnicity. (See Figure 5.1.) This required a careful analysis of the factors that pertain to ethnicity and a determination of how best to quantify them. Broad and inclusive subscales were constructed to measure the ethnic relatedness of culture, nationality, and religion, the sum total of which represent a measure of ethnic cohesiveness. It was also important to develop a social class construct as a means of identifying socioeconomic differences within the Polish-American community. (See Table 4.2.)

THE RESEARCH PROBLEM

The critical research problem is the need to examine current and predicted ethnic identity in America, especially as it pertains to Polish-Americans and specifically those living in the Los Angeles Metropolitan Area. This is important because if this country continues to be a nation of subgroups, at least for the next generation or two, it will be necessary to assess public policies and programs, taking into account the presumed "holding power" of ethnicity. It is also necessary to examine the socioeconomic element to determine whether the rising affluence of society, including that of Polonia, will affect ethnicity.

The problem of adverse stereotypes was a related consideration in terms of its impact on group continuity. If Polish identification is associated with low status the future of the group may be very tenuous, particularly among the younger generations. This may be seen in the context of cognitive dissonance, a psychologically uncomfortable condition that gives rise to pressures to reduce it (Festinger, 1962).

---

*"Group cohesiveness" is the importance of a group to its members; this refers especially to the maintenance of group boundaries (Borhek, 1970).

A further consideration was the need to trace the different kinds of residential patterns that have been developed by the Polish ethnic group in the Los Angeles area. It was important, therefore, to assess the impact of the relative lack of primary group contact on its ethnic cohesiveness and to ascertain to what extent it has been able to substitute other means of in-group reinforcement.

RESEARCH HYPOTHESES

Within the framework of the foregoing theory and research question it was felt that the salience of ethnicity could be measured empirically and that differences could be observed among the various groupings. Consequently, the research question was explored through two statistical approaches, each requiring a different research hypothesis; both hypotheses were tested in the null form.

Research Hypothesis A (generational groups): There is a significant difference between levels of ethnic identity as measured by the group cohesiveness scale, with ethnic identity tending to diminish over generations according to the "straight line" theory.

Research Hypothesis B (social class groups): There is a significant difference between levels of ethnic identity as measured by the group cohesiveness scale, with ethnicity tending to vary inversely with social class.

THE USEFULNESS OF THIS STUDY

In view of the limited availability of previous work in this area it is felt that the current study improves on earlier investigations in the following ways:

1. With the development of a group cohesiveness scale this study provides a needed tool for measuring ethnic differences among Polish-Americans.
2. The belief that the scale can be readily adapted for use with other groups leads to the possibility of a common methodological approach to the various ethnic groups; in this way meaningful comparisons can be made over periods of time.
3. The analysis that led to the creation of the scale contributes to a definition of ethnic identity through a careful assessment of the relevant variables.
4. The study compares generational and social class groups empirically.
5. An empirical means is offered for predicting the future of ethnic cohesiveness.

6.   A basis is provided for making more meaningful social policy deci-
     sions, especially for public and private agencies concerned with
     improving intergroup relations.

THE ORGANIZATION OF THIS BOOK

Chapter 1 sets forth the background and orientation that describe the
need for research on ethnic identity. The research problem and the theoretical
basis for the study are delineated.

Chapter 2 assesses the experiences that affected the adjustment of Polish
immigrants to America. The development of ethnic structures and the Polish
settlement in California and Los Angeles are discussed.

Chapter 3 looks at the cultural, religious, and national aspects of ethnic
identification. Social class and generational factors are also related to ethnicity.

Chapter 4 outlines the research design, the procedure, the sample, and the
statistical techniques and relates them to the research questions.

Chapter 5 presents the outcome of the data analyses and the examination
of the hypotheses.

Chapter 6 includes a discussion of the findings and contains the evaluative
interpretations, conclusions, and recommendations on the future of ethnicity.

2

THE MIGRATION
FROM POLAND TO AMERICA

THE POLISH IMMIGRATION AND
CURRENT POPULATION STATISTICS

An estimation of the Polish-American population at 6 million persons was derived from a number of sources. One of these was the National Opinion Research Center (NORC) Study (Greeley and Rossi, 1968), in which Polish Catholics were found to be 10 percent of all born Catholics in the national population, according to the ethnic background of the father. If this is applied to the 1960 statistics, which showed 42,104,900 Roman Catholics (Rosten, 1963), there would be an estimated 4,200,000 Roman Catholic Polish-Americans. Added to this are nearly 300,000 members of the Polish National Catholic Church in America (PNC) and a small but undetermined number of others of Protestant background or unaffiliated. With the general growth of the population in the last decade these figures must now be substantially increased.

Another way of calculating the number of Polish-Americans is by using the figures of Bogue (1959), which placed the Roman Catholic population at 25.7 percent of the total. As related to the current figure of some 210 million people in the United States, there are approximately 54 million Roman Catholics. The NORC report of a 10 percent Polish Roman Catholic population would have provided an estimated 5.4 million; with the addition of the PNC, Protestants, and unaffiliated persons the total is approximately 6 million Polish-Americans. This does not include Jews of Polish ancestry, many of whom are part of the Polish foreign stock grouping of the U.S. Census.* It is

---

*As used by the Census, the term "foreign stock" includes both the foreign-born and the native-born of foreign or mixed parentage. This groups is often referred to as "foreign white stock" (Bogue, 1959).

important to note, however, that the current study is focused entirely on non-Jewish Poles.

Although census figures are helpful in locating present population and tracing ongoing trends pertaining to foreign stock, by excluding figures on the third, fourth, and subsequent generations they give only a partial picture of the ethnic communities. Table 2.1 summarizes the data available on foreign stock from 1860 to 1970. It shows that the number of foreign-born increased until 1930 and has declined steadily since then, but that, despite some variations, the native white population of foreign or mixed parentage has remained fairly constant since 1930.

TABLE 2.1

Nativity and Mother Tongue of Polish Foreign Stock in the United States

Year	Total Foreign White Stock	Foreign-born White[a]	Native White of Foreign or Mixed Parentage[b]	Mother Tongue of the Foreign-born[d]
1860		7,298		
1870		14,436		
1880		48,557		
1890		147,440		
1900	710,171	383,407	326,764	
1910	1,663,808	937,884[c]	725,924	943,871
1920	2,443,330	1,139,979	1,303,351	1,077,392
1930	3,342,198	1,268,583	2,073,615	965,899
1940	2,905,859	993,479	1,912,380	801,680
1950	2,786,199	861,184	1,925,015	
1960	2,780,026	747,950	2,032,076	581,936
1970	2,374,244	584,107	1,826,137	419,912

[a]Prior to 1910 the data refer to "foreign-born" persons; from 1910 on they refer to "foreign-born white." Because of the virtual absence of a non-White population in Poland there is no significant impact on these figures (Bogue, 1959; Hutchinson, 1956).

[b]Persons classified as of "mixed foreign parentage" for the years prior to 1930 have been distributed according to the country of birth of the father.

[c]These were deducted from the numbers of immigrants from Germany, Austria, and Russia and consist largely of those who list Polish as their mother tongue.

[d]A number of persons born in Poland identify languages other than Polish as their "mother tongue."

Source: U.S. Census of Population: 1960, Vol 1, Part 1; Historical Statistics of the U.S., Colonial Times to 1957; United States Censuses of 1870, 1880, 1900, 1920, 1930, 1940, 1950, and 1970.

A recent and undoubtedly more accurate census was conducted in November 1969 through a sample survey on country of origin. For the first time in a U.S. Census, individuals reported the ethnic association they felt most strongly. Of these, 4,021,000 identified themselves as of Polish origin (Population Characteristics, 1971); this points to a considerably larger number than the 1970 census figure for total Polish foreign stock of 2,374,244, which consists only of the foreign-born and those of foreign or mixed parentage. It was also observed that 2,018,026 persons of all generations said their mother tongue was Polish (Bureau of the U.S. Census, 1972).

Census figures have been questioned by Polish sources who asserted that the number of Polish-Americans was much higher. A 1955 study presented to the Polish American Congress by Dr. Ladislaus Korczynski, estimated the number at 7,000,000, but the organization itself reported 6,372,000 through a tally of census data, church records, and statistics of fraternal and social groups (Polish American Congress, 1957). Joseph A. Wytrwal (1969) estimated well over 10,000,000, and he contended that if the fourth and fifth generations had been included the number would have been somewhere around 15,000,000.

Although these figures seem unreasonably high, it is undoubtedly true that many individuals were missed by the census. One reason was that until 1918 Poland was an occupied country and many Poles coming to the United States were therefore counted as Germans, Austrians, or Russians. Felix Thomas Seroczynski (1911) noted that by 1900, of the more than one-third of a million foreign-born Poles in America, 39 percent were from Germany, 40 percent from Russia, and 15 percent from Austria-Hungary.

Later census figures based on the mother tongue of the immigrants may also have been low because the respondents did not wish to identify themselves as Polish. The accuracy of the census data was further reduced by such circumstances as changes in census practices, shifts of national boundaries, and the fact that many Lithuanians declared themselves as Poles in the nineteenth century (Hutchinson, 1956; Szynczak, 1964).

Although most of this immigration took place between 1890 and 1914, Poles were a part of the American tradition from the time of the Jamestown settlement in 1608. Miecislaus Haiman (1939) divided the history of Polish immigration into three periods:

1. The Colonial Immigration from 1608 to 1776, which consisted primarily of adventurers and soldiers of fortune.
2. The Political Immigration from 1776 to 1865, which included some aristocrats and other political exiles seeking freedom.
3. The Economic Immigration from 1865 to 1939, which was largely peasants seeking opportunity. Until Poland regained its freedom in 1918 this was also to some extent political because of the oppression of the occupying powers.

Another category of immigrants arrived under the Refugee Relief Acts following World War II; this was essentially a more educated group, consisting of displaced persons, refugees, and others, some seeking economic opportunity but most looking for political freedom.* By 1960 those who had arrived since 1940 represented 31.7 percent of the total Polish foreign-born population, representing an increasing proportion of the newer immigrants (Taeuber and Taeuber, 1967). The ability of these highly motivated people to speak English, combined with their cultural background, has enabled a large number of them to reach a middle- or upper-class income (Mostwin, 1969).

This shift in the composition of present-day immigration represented a change in national policy from the acceptance of predominantly unskilled labor prior to World War II to a focus on those with specialized skills and professional qualifications. The new U.S. policy signified an abandonment of the discriminatory national-origins basis of quotas that had been instituted in 1917 and subsequent years in order to curtail immigration from Europe, particularly from the "less desirable" eastern, central, and southern parts (Hutchinson, 1966; Maisel, 1955).

THE BACKGROUND OF THE POLISH PEASANT

The peasants who came to America at the turn of the century were largely unaware of the significance of the Polish historical experience. Religious traditions, educational patterns, and exposure to invading armies had their part in the shaping of Polish culture.

Influenced by the early Byzantine and Roman civilizations, Poland was profoundly affected by the introduction of Christianity in 962 A.D. A steadfast and virtually total religious commitment to Rome has been maintained to this day despite the force of the Reformation, occupation by numerous conquerors, and even the current domination of an anti-religious Communist government. Indeed, the Poles, particularly among the aristocracy, have enjoyed religious and political freedom and freedom of conscience in many periods of their history.

The national consciousness and ethnic solidarity of the Poles goes back at least to the fifteenth century and was due in large measure to the cohesiveness of the Polish nobility. Art, religion, literature, and science were utilized for the unification and preservation of Polish life and culture, and the national ideal was exalted above everything else.

> Poland was a republic when other nations were rigid monarchies. Poland had a relatively perfect system of national representation which was in conformity with her advanced political development.

---

*"Displaced persons" were Europeans who were rendered homeless by World War II and who for various reasons could not with safety resume residence in their prewar communities (Marden and Meyer, 1968).

Poland had a Senate and a House of Representatives as early as the latter part of the 14th century. She had her minor Diets where representatives were chosen. Already at that early period the Polish government represented the closest prototype of the American government. (Zielinski, 1933, p. 97.)

In the eighteenth century, however, Poland declined steadily under the rule of the Saxon kings, and by 1795 it was partitioned among Prussia, Austria, and Russia. Culture and learning were sharply de-emphasized, and public education continued to be almost nonexistent until the nineteenth century; even then it was limited and poor. Schools were used largely as instruments of Russification or Germanization, and the development of Polish culture, language, and national feelings was drastically curtailed as efforts were made to assimilate Poles into other national cultures.

Consequently, Poland's history dating from 1795 was dominated by the crushing burden of occupation, and it was not until the victory of the Allies in 1918 that her unity and independence were restored. This was short-lived, however; Poland was occupied once again following the Nazi invasion in 1939. Even the Allied victory of World War II failed to restore complete independence as a result of the subsequent dominance of the USSR over the "iron curtain" nations (Super, 1939; Wytrwal, 1961).

For the Polish peasant, the virtual lack of political rights until the end of the eighteenth century and the subsequent limitations imposed by the occupying powers contributed to a perception of the political realm as a mysterious entity that was beyond his ability to change.

William I. Thomas and Florian Znaniecki (1918-20) completed the picture of the Polish peasant group by describing it as a concrete, ethnically homogeneous society developed over many generations. There was little involvement in the higher forms of cultural productivity despite a Polish intellectual tradition dating from the establishment of the University in Cracow in 1364, an institution served by such brilliant scholars as Nicholas Copernicus.

As for the religious life of the peasant, it consisted not only of the practices and doctrines of the Church but also of a world of good and evil spirits, a belief in witchcraft, and other folkways that transcended religious orthodoxy. The village parish itself was the center of family and communal life, and religion was interwoven with the pragmatic interests and requirements of everyday existence.

Class distinctions tended to be very rigid, particularly between the peasants and the gentry, as a result of the presence of serfdom over many centuries. Nonetheless, the peasants were influenced by others including the clergy, the nobility, and the working and middle classes of the cities. The peasants were lacking in leadership and limited in education, both by the relative absence of educational institutions and by a traditional opposition to substantial formal learning. Through the press, however, a nationwide social opinion was created and the peasant class was ultimately helped to rise to a higher cultural level.

The traditional Polish peasant family was a primary social group in which the relations of husband and wife were controlled by both the united families. Family norms included respect, obedience, and fidelity, as well as those dictated by economic considerations. It was a system of mutual obligations and requirements in which the success or failure of the individual was related to the status of the family.

In sum, the peasant had lived in a permanent, slow-changing, agricultural community for hundreds of years. His social milieu provided him with stability, continuity, and control, and when there was an unexpected occurrence he relied on his family and group for support. Until recently he had been a member of a politically and culturally passive class with relatively little involvement in the major institutions of society.

THE ADJUSTMENT PROCESS IN AMERICA

This was the orientation of most of those who constituted the large wave of Polish immigration to the United States in the late nineteenth and early twentieth centuries. It was a mass migration that ultimately provided opportunities for the peasants to move into the lower-middle and middle classes, usually through a painful and difficult process of disorganization and reorganization in an environment that was often hostile (Thomas and Znaniecki, 1918-20).

Unable to speak English, uneducated, and often exploited, these immigrants were primarily laborers in jobs at the bottom of the ladder. Strong, hard-working, and conscientious, they were employed in the unskilled occupations of the textile mills of New England, the mines of Pennsylvania, the steel mills of Ohio, the slaughter houses of Chicago, the railroads and lumber mills of the West, and ultimately in the automobile plants of Michigan. While small numbers ventured into farming, it was the better wages of industry that attracted most of these workers; at the same time, native Americans were also leaving the farms for the cities at this time. (Jones, 1960; Wytrwal, 1961).

There was a wide social and cultural gap between the immigrants and the dominant segments of society in the United States that often produced confusion and disruption among the newcomers. Cut off from the familiar stratified environment of their villages, they felt the need to identify with others like themselves, particularly in a setting where a heightened self-awareness was being expressed by other alien groups. The Poles tended to live in close physical proximity to each other, deriving comfort and satisfaction from their common language, religion, and mutual recollection of old experiences. This led to the growth of services and voluntary associations, and contributed to a Polish national consciousness to which they had generally been indifferent in Poland, where they had been oriented to a life around the village parish.

In America many of the immigrants became active Polish patriots with a great desire to do something for their former land, and a romanticized notion of Poland emerged as a place of heroes and glorious causes. While many still referred to themselves in terms of their old villages or sections of occupied Poland, a cohesive Polish-American group gradually evolved called Polonia, which was neither Polish nor American, but rather a marginal society with its own unique rationale and institutions (Swastek, 1944; Wytrwal, 1961).

It was the small Polish intellectual leadership, however, rather than the peasant population, that was able to communicate a consciousness of the common cultural heritage and develop the nationalism that became the main force unifying Poles in America. According to Helena Znaniecki Lopata (1964) this was a deterrent to assimilation, since it was possible for a member to meet all of his needs within the confines of the group without speaking English. The development of Polish nationalism, the formation of numerous voluntary associations concerned with ethnic preservation, the ability to transmit the culture to new generations through schools and the Church, and the revival of interest in Polish culture—all contributed to slowing the rate of assimilation. Nonetheless changes occurred, and there was a shift from a Polish to a Polish-American orientation.

THE ETHNIC SOCIETIES OF POLONIA

As Father Joseph Swastek (1952) indicated, there were four characteristic institutions of Polonia that served as foundations upon which the immigrants built their lives: the parish church, the school, the press, and the ethnic society. Of particular importance were the ethnic societies, which evolved slowly because originally there were no strong ties among those who came from different parts of Poland or who settled in different parts of America.

In the early years assistance was based on individual collections for the benefit of the sick or poor, but eventually an organized self-help program was developed in the form of the mutual aid society. Thomas and Znaniecki (1918-20) noted that charity was considered a disgrace if it came from American institutions. Moreover, the very fact that mutual assistance was necessary showed that the old communal solidarity of the peasant village, where each individual had a claim on the help of all the others without the need for such associations, had been modified in the new milieu.

The first such group was the Polish Committee, founded in 1834, but it was of short duration (Haiman, 1939). A more permanent body was organized in Chicago in 1864; in time this also became a social club and community center. A large hall was built, filled with tables and chairs, and used for Polish folk dancing, music, and drama. This became the model for later meeting-places, which were usually called Polish Homes.

In 1873 Father Gieryk of Detroit attempted to create a superterritorial institution, a national body that would bring together representatives of the various Polish colonies to manage the affairs of American Poles. This was an association of priests representing parishes, and it failed, primarily because there were not enough Polish priests to provide the needed leadership. It also did not take into account the strong secular element of Polish-American communal development, which resisted religious domination.

Subsequently a new leadership emerged, concerned both with the acculturation of Polonia and the desire to maintain some interest in Poland's cultural attainments and political independence. Working through a complex of local and national organizations, the new leaders sought to preserve Polish traditions and to provide for mutual assistance in time of need.

The Polish National Alliance (PNA) was founded in 1880 as a means of bringing together various local Polish associations in different communities. These associations had as their aims economic, hedonistic, political, religious, aesthetic, and intellectual matters (Thomas and Znaniecki, 1918-20). The specific aims of the PNA included promotion of education and immigration, provision of assistance based on insurance, and protection of the interests of Polish-Americans. Its central goal was to develop unified support for the Polish national struggle for freedom while at the same time encouraging active participation in and loyalty to America.

The Polish Roman Catholic Union (PRCU) was formed a few months later because the Polish clergy felt that the rising PNA might be dangerous to the exclusive supremacy that the clergy had hitherto enjoyed (Wytrwal, 1961). The PRCU focused on the cultural identity of the Polish-American community rather than on the needs of Poland, emphasizing ethnic separateness and discouraging participation in American institutions. Its objectives included preserving the autonomy of the Polish Roman Catholic Church and the preservation of the integrity of Polish parishes by preventing their absorption into the Irish-dominated Catholic hierarchy in America. In order to compete with the PNA the PRCU had to develop an insurance program and other philanthropic services. Like the PNA it was a superstructure wherein membership was granted not to individuals but to groups or societies. Although there was bitter antagonism between them in the early days because the PNA stressed Polish needs and the PRCU had a more American approach, in time the differences blurred and a cohesiveness and mutual cooperation emerged based on Polish-American interests and cemented by their interlocking memberships.

Over the years other national societies were created, most seeking to fulfill the social and cultural expectations of their members and to provide insurance. These associations tried to do a little of everything, and became almost parishes in miniature. The Polish Falcons was established in 1888; it emphasized physical fitness and military training for patriotic service to America and to the cause of Polish freedom (Wytrwal, 1961). The Polish Women's Alliance of America was formed in 1898 for the promotion of patriotism and welfare, both in the United States and Poland. In addition to fostering "Polish ideals" in the younger generation, it also provided insurance benefits as a mutual aid society (Polish Women's Alliance, 1963). The Alliance of Polish Socialists, however, rejected the concept of ethnic solidarity, seeking to promote the cause of socialism in cooperation with non-Poles (Thomas and Znaniecki, 1918-20). And what is surprising in light of the strong anti-Communist feelings of

Polonia is that a small but active Communist group flourished in Ham-tramck, a Polish enclave near Detroit (Wood, 1955).

Opposition to Communism was best exemplified in the programs of the Polish American Congress, which sought to combat its growth both here and abroad and to work for the restoration of freedom in Poland. Convened in 1944, the Congress brought together representatives of Polonia to inform the American public of Polish contributions, to aid in the resettlement of displaced persons, to organize Polish-Americans for unity, and to further cultural and civic development (Karcz, 1959; Polish American Congress, 1957).

Lopata (1964) hypothesized that there were three basic functions of the ethnic association: (1) forming within the community as a distinct but flexible unit, (2) developing a close relationship between Polonia and Poland, and (3) improving the relationship between Polonia and American society. Since the 1920s, however, and even more vigorously today, the major aim of a number of these groups has been to eliminate discrimination against Poles in America and to improve their status. There has also been a need to formulate an ideology that would justify the continuity of Polonia, appeal to the interests of the changing Polish-American, and offer a means of assuring group survival. The underlying assumption has been that the social, economic, and political life of America is influenced substantially by the pressures of powerful, organized, ethnic subgroups. Consequently these associations have appeared to offer the individual improvement of his own condition through improvement of the status of the entire subgroup. This ideology has contributed to the creation of a common culture aimed at enhancing the self-image of Polonia and educating American society to its importance.

Today Americans of Polish descent have approximately 10,000 fraternal, dramatic, literary, musical, social, cultural, religious, and athletic societies all over the country. Many are branches or affiliates of the national organizations, whose total membership is more than 800,000. It is estimated that there are 831 Polish Roman Catholic parishes, 553 elementary schools, 71 high schools, 6 colleges, 4 seminaries, 34 hospitals, and 146 other institutions funded by Polish-Americans and staffed by some 2,000 priests and large numbers of nuns and lay people of Polish ancestry. There are 5 daily newspapers published in the Polish language, which, together with numerous weeklies, monthlies, and periodicals, represent a circulation of nearly 750,000, one of the largest foreign-language media groups in the United States (Wytrwal, 1969). A further analysis of the influence of the parish church, the school, and the press will be presented in Chapter 3.

POLISH SETTLEMENT IN CALIFORNIA

Current scholars on ethnicity have been relatively unaware that early Polish immigration included a large number of pioneers. According to the U.S.

Census there were 730 foreign-born Poles in California in 1860, some 10 percent of the total of 7,298 Polish immigrants in America.

Although later Polish settlements were primarily in the cities of the East and Midwest, many Poles participated in the early development of America's western frontier. These included political exiles and intellectuals who were freely admitted to American society and who tended to assimilate rapidly. Some of them were lukewarm toward the Catholic faith and preferred to be looked on as Liberals and Nationalists. They were distributed in every state and territory of the Union including California, where the small number of individuals who had settled earlier was increased by the Gold Rush of 1850 (Wytrwal, 1961).

The first Polish center in California was at San Francisco and consisted of refugees fleeing the revolutions of 1830 and 1848 (Kosberg, 1952). Some Poles reached California through Alaska when it was a Russian colony; among them was Dionisius Zaremba, the sea captain who transacted the sale of Fort Ross to Sutter in 1845. A member of the Donner party, which met disaster in the Sierra Nevadas in 1846, was James F. Reed, whose father was of Polish birth and had changed his name from Rydnowski (Kowalczyk, 1948).

Among the most famous Polish pioneers of California was Paul Wierzbicki, who was deported to America in 1834 because of his participation in the 1830 insurrection and who came to the state in 1847. After traveling for four months on foot and horse through the Gold Region he wrote a pamphlet titled "California As It Is, and As It May Be, or A Guide to the Gold Region." This was the first English book printed at San Francisco or anywhere west of the Rockies and it still considered an important account of early California. Wierzbicki also helped to organize the first medical society in San Francisco and authored the first paper on the history of medicine in California (Haiman, 1939, 1940; Wytrwal, 1961).

Although most of the early settlement was in San Francisco and Northern California, a small but important colony was established in Anaheim in 1876 by a group of eleven Polish intellectuals and artists under the leadership of the actress Madame Helena Modjeska. Among the participants in this communal effort, which was modeled after Brook Farm, was the author Henryk Sienkiewicz.

While the experiment of these impractical romantics lasted only eighteen months, Madame Modjeska continued to maintain her home in nearby Santiago Canyon. Until she died in 1909, and until the pianist and composer Paderewski gave up his ranch in Paso Robles in 1914 to return to Europe, their homes were gathering places for Polish and non-Polish intellectuals. The site of Madame Modjeska's estate is referred to as Modjeska Canyon, and a peak in the Santa Ana Mountains is named in her honor. Five generations of the Modjeska family have made their homes in Southern California, including her son Ralph, a bridge builder who participated in the planning and building of the Golden Gate Bridge (Kosberg, 1952).

Over the years Poles have continued to move to California, mostly to the Southern part, although their percentage of the total population of the state has declined markedly. As indicated in Table 2.2, there has been a substantial growth of the Polish-American population in California since World War II, with the 1970 census reporting a total of 115,584 foreign white stock of Polish origin. Since the census did not record those of the third or subsequent generations it is likely that there were many more people of Polish ancestry in California.

A breakdown of the 1970 figures indicates that there were 31,381 Polish foreign-born and 84,203 native whites of foreign or mixed Polish parentage. Those foreign-born who claimed Polish as their mother tongue numbered 19,943, suggesting that a considerable number of the 31,381 foreign-born and a smaller number of the native-born were Jews of Polish nationality whose mother tongue was Yiddish. In addition to the foreign-born there were 39,586 natives of foreign or mixed parentage and 22,892 natives of native

TABLE 2.2

Nativity and Mother Tongue of Polish Foreign Stock in California

Year	Total Foreign White Stock	Foreign-born	Native White of Foreign or Mixed Parentage	Mother Tongue of the Foreign-born[a]
1860		730		
1870		804		
1880		1,026		
1890		914		
1900		1,320		
1910		3,542[b]		3,595
1920		7,082		4,908
1930		14,290		7,339
1940	37,035	14,735	22,300	7,780
1950	72,096	23,776	48,320	
1960	110,086	31,877	78,209	21,304
1970	115,584	31,381	84,203	19,943

[a]A number of persons born in Poland identify languages other than Polish as their "mother tongue."

[b]These were deducted from the figures on immigrants from Germany, Austria, and Russia and consist largely of those who list Polish as their mother tongue.

Source: *1950 Census of Population, California*, vol. 2, part 5; *U.S. Census of Population: 1960, California*, Final Report PC(1)-6D; *1960 Census of Population, California*, "Country of Origin of the Foreign Stock, for the State, Urban and Rural, 1960, and 1910 to 1940," vol. 1, part 6; Censuses of 1870, 1880, 1900, 1920, 1930, 1940, 1950, and 1970.

parentage, a California total of 82,421 persons who indicated Polish as their mother tongue.

Of special interest is the fact that the Polish-Americans who settled in the West are much better educated than those in the rest of the country. For individuals fourteen years of age or older the median number of school years completed for the native-born of foreign or mixed parentage is 12.2. This compares with a national Polish median of 10.7 years. The Polish foreing-born who reside in the West have 8.7 years of education as compared with a national median of 6.9 years (U.S. Census, 1960).

These figures suggest the likelihood that those who are better educated tend to be more mobile. They also indicate that the Polish-American residents of the West, many of whom live in Southern California, represent a group of higher socioeconomic status than the national population of Polonia, which is largely working-class.

THE POLISH-AMERICAN POPULATION OF LOS ANGELES

Thomas and Znaniecki (1918-20) noted that while the majority of Poles gathered around their churches and schools, many were scattered because they lived near where they worked. Hence it was only when there were enough Poles living in an area that a Polish parish was formed. This observation appears to be particularly relevant to the experience of Polonia in Los Angeles, where there were only a few hundred Poles in the nineteenth century, living in widely dispersed areas. Since there was no Polish parish the growing colony took advantage of a visit by Father Organisciak in 1908 to hold Polish Masses in a borrowed church facility in Eagle Rock. Aimed at the creation of a Polish parish, this experiment failed because of the long distances people had to travel (Strakacz, 1958).

Although a small Polish enclave developed in East Los Angeles, the wide dispersion of the population in 1920 is indicated by the data in Table 2.3 (U.S. Bureau of the Census, 1922).

The 1960 census (U.S. Bureau of the Census, 1967) reported a continued widespread dispersion of the population, with Polish foreign stock residing in 632 of the 710 Census tracts in the City of Los Angeles and representing a total of 44,198 persons. A breakdown of these figures indicates some relatively small concentrations in different parts of the city, in the context of a pattern of broad distribution. There were 78 Census tracts with no Polish foreign stock, 506 tracts with under 100 persons, 98 tracts with between 100 and 249 persons, 18 tracts with between 250 and 499 persons, and 10 tracts with 500 or more persons.

As indicated in the tables in the Appendix, Polish foreign stock was represented in all of the separately incorporated communities within the Los Angeles-Long Beach Standard Metropolitan Statistical Area (SMSA). The figure for this SMSA was 73,959, of whom 31,877 were foreign-born

TABLE 2.3

Foreign-born White Poles in the City of Los Angeles in 1920

Assembly District	Number of People
61	127
62	8
63	211
64	433
65	119
66	250
69	1
70	0
71	192
72	188
73	322
74	151
75	203
Total	2,205

Source: Fourteenth Census of the United States, 1920 (Washington, D.C.: Government Printing Office, 1922).

and 42,082 were native white of foreign or mixed parentage (U.S. Census, 1960).

Polish-Americans were also widely distributed throughout Los Angeles and Orange Counties, with the latter having a Polish foreign stock of 3,501 persons. The 1,050 persons in Burbank were in all of the 18 Census tracts; the 2,084 persons in Long Beach were in 62 of the 71 tracts, and a high concentration of 1,700 persons was noted in the 5 tracts of West Hollywood. Polish foreign stock was still represented in 15 of the 17 tracts in East Los Angeles, an area of early settlement that is now largely Mexican-American. It is interesting to note that 39,477 persons in the Los Angeles-Long Beach SMSA claimed Polish as their mother tongue, including 11,974 foreign-born, 18,508 native of foreign or mixed parentage, and 8,995 native of native parentage (U.S. Bureau of the Census, 1970).

Until the Polish Home was built in 1924 at 4200 Avalon Boulevard, many Poles attended services at St. Vibiana's Cathedral. The first Polish Mass held in the new Home was celebrated by the Reverend Bronislaw Krzeminski, and services were held there until 1926, when a chapel was purchased from another denomination at 52nd Street and Towne Avenue.

The church, which was called Christ the King, received approval from Archbishop Cantwell of Los Angeles.

In 1944 the congregation purchased the estate of Fatty Arbuckle at 3424 West Adams Boulevard and created a chapel in an existing structure until enough money was available to build the present church on this property. Named Our Lady of the Bright Mount (Matka Boska Czestochowska), it was dedicated in 1956 as a national parish serving the Polish community under the authority of the Archdiocese (Strakacz, 1958). This was the only Polish Roman Catholic parish established west of the Rockies. In 1932 it was one of 1,140 Polish parishes in America (Szynczak, 1964), and today it is one of 831 (Wytrwal, 1969).

At one time there was an attempt to develop a Polish-language parochial school, but it failed because the parishioners lived in different parts of the metropolitan area and the children were not able to go to school on a daily basis. Today there is a Saturday all-day school at the church, where 45 children learn the Polish language, history, and culture. Some 460 families, or nearly 2,000 individuals, are members of the church, and others who are nonmembers provide support. Three Masses are held every Sunday, and on important holidays as many as five Masses are held. It is estimated that some 2,000 persons come to the church for Christmas and Easter services. The present pastor is Father Stanislaw Jureko, who succeeded Father Krzeminski (Rydzeski, 1971).

Guardian Angel Polish National Catholic Church (PNC) was established in Los Angeles in 1959; this is the only PNC church west of the Rockies. The PNC was organized in 1904 by Polish-American Catholics who were seeking a larger voice in American Catholicism, greater ethnic decentralization of the Church, and separate control over church properties. (Greene, 1966.) Although small numbers of Lithuanians and other non-Poles are members of the PNC its hierarchy is entirely Polish. It has 140 churches in the United States with an estimated membership of 282,411 (Wytrwal, 1969). The current pastor of the Los Angeles parish of some 100 families which was organized by the Late Father Sienkiewicz, is the Reverend Edward Kalata. Informal contact is maintained with the Polish Roman Catholic Church, although they are separate bodies locally and nationally (Kalata, 1970).

In 1950 a directory indicated that there were thirty Polish-American groups in the Los Angeles area including Councils of the PNA and PRCU; the Polish Women's Alliance; the Polish Literary and Dramatic Circle; the Polish University Club; organizations concerned with veterans, labor, and business and professional people; and cultural and intellectual activities (Polish American Congress, 1950). This listing did not identify the numerous groups associated with the Polish parish, which, if included separately, would have added substantially to the total. Some of the groups listed used the facilities of the Polish churches, while others gathered at the Polish Auditorium, a social and meeting hall located at 4434 Crenshaw Boulevard.

For a number of years a local newspaper called *The Panorama of Polonia* was published once a month. It was temporarily discontinued several years ago after the death of the publisher, but it is again being published. The national daily paper *Dziennik Zwiazkowy*, which is distributed by the PNA, has a weekly California edition providing news of interest to the Los Angeles Polonia. There are, however, no local radio or television programs relating to the Polish community (Rydzeski, 1971).

3

THE MEANING
OF ETHNIC IDENTITY

This chapter presents an overview of previous writings and studies pertaining to the diverse aspects of ethnicity and relevant to the generational and social-class factors identified in the theory structure.

ETHNICITY, ASSIMILATION, AND PLURALISM

The concept of group determination of behavior was an old focus in sociology that suggested men acted according to the social frame of reference of their groups. Robert K. Merton (1957) observed that the attitudes and behavior of people can also be shaped by groups other than their own. Further, while one may be a member of many reference groups including those of occupation, religion, ethnic origin, and social class, the primary environment takes precedence when there is a conflict.

Oscar Handlin (1951), Glazer and Moynihan (1970), and others believe that differences in origin affect many aspects of communal life, and they point to the influence of ethnicity on the social, economic, and political milieu. Conversely, a number of ethnic groups have been transformed by the American experience and re-created as new and identifiable entities according to unique circumstances of time, place, and culture.

Gordon (1964) narrowed the focus of Reference Group Theory by suggesting that ethnicity and social class are the principal factors contributing to the subculture of American life. He hypothesized that persons of the same social class but of different ethnic groups share behavioral similarities but not a sense of peoplehood. Those of the same ethnic group but of a different social class share a sense of peoplehood but not behavioral similarities. As indicated in the second section of Chapter 1, those who share both were described as an "ethclass."

An analytical typology was developed that identified several systems of assimilation. Anglo-conformity demanded the complete renunciation of the immigrants' ancestral culture and the substitution of the behavior and values of middle class WASPs, America's core "ethclass." This was the dominant and almost universally accepted model of assimilation, the goal of which was to break up subgroups and implant "American" concepts and patterns. The other systems of assimilation were the "melting pot" and "cultural pluralism" theories referred to earlier.

While recognizing that biological amalgamation is taking place and that groups are also acculturating according to the model of Anglo-conformity, Gordon pointed to an important distinction between cultural and structural pluralism. He observed that we are assimilating culturally while maintaining separate structures that provide a framework for group existence. These include the organizations, families, and informal friendship patterns so vital to the continuation of an ethnic communal life.

Another view of assimilation was advanced by Ruby Jo Kennedy (1944) and popularized by Will Herberg (1960). Although accepting the fact of racial pluralism they suggest that assimilation is taking place along religious lines in a "triple melting pot." They believe there is a tendency for people to marry within their own religious group, particularly in the third generation of the descendants of immigrants, except for Negroes, Orientals, and others who are identifiable racially. Thus they feel that the distinctions among the white ethnic groups are disappearing as Italian Catholics marry Polish Catholics, East European Jews marry German Jews, and WASPs amalgamate with Scandinavians and other Protestants.

This view was challenged by Greeley (1969) and others, who deplored the fact that Americans devote too little attention to the ethnic groups that still flourish in our society. He felt that the "triple melting pot" judgment was premature and that people still seek their intimate friends and marriage partners within their own ethnic groups. As an example he pointed to the continuing antagonism between the Poles and the Irish, which is not resolved by the Catholic religion common to both.

The predicted decline of ethnicity was also challenged by Glazer and Moynihan in a reassessment of their own earlier view of the assimilationist tendencies of white ethnic groups:

Beyond the accidents of history, one suspects, is the reality that human groups endure, and that they provide some satisfaction to their members, and that the adoption of a totally new ethnic identity, by dropping whatever one is to become simply American, is inhibited by strong elements in the social structure of the United States. It is inhibited by a subtle system of identifying, which ranges from brutal discrimination and prejudice to merely naming. It is inhibited by the unavailability of a simple "American" identity. One is a New Englander, or a Southerner, or a mid-Westerner, and all these things mean something too concrete for the ethnic to adopt completely, while excluding his ethnic identity. (Glazer and Moynihan, 1970, pp. xxxiii and xxxiv).

Consequently, three new hypotheses were set forth about the continuing significance of ethnicity:

1. With the downgrading of the occupational identification of the working class, the prestige in being a member of an ethnic group has become greater.
2. The sources of ethnic identification have been found more in the American experience than in the European national homeland.
3. Contrary to the Herberg hypothesis, religion has not displaced ethnic identification.

Additional support has been given to the concept of ethnic pluralism by those who stress the belief that America is made up of self-interested groups rather than an integrated community of individuals.

> ... the widespread existence of such subcommunities and their importance have made our society vastly more complex than our ideas of town-hall democracy would allow us to believe. In one set of circumstances we strive to live up to the principle "regardless of" race, color, and creed; in other circumstances, *race, color,* and *creed* are the very principles by which human relationships are organized. (Danzig, 1968, p. 18.)

THE ETHNIC DIMENSION

As indicated in the third section of Chapter 1, a group cohesiveness scale has been created to measure the salience of ethnicity among Polish-Americans. After consultation with authoritative sources and a review of the literature, three subscales on the ethnic aspects of religion, culture, and nationality were constructed, the sum total of which represented a broad-gauged measure of ethnicity. The following discussion is related to this general framework.

Louis Wirth (1964) suggested that the development of ethnicity is based largely on the religious, linguistic, and cultural heritage of the group, its drive to obtain recognition and toleration of these differences, and the quest for economic and political equality. Lloyd W. Warner (1953) saw the ethnic church not only as a repository of the sacred values and symbols of the group but as a framework for organizing its national and cultural attitudes and a link to the ancestral national home. The close connection between religion, nationality, and culture was also noted by Joseph S. Roucek and Francis J. Brown (1937), Lopata (1964), and as follows by Arthur Evans Wood (1955):

If, therefore, one were to summarize the various motives involved in the organized social life of the community, one would cite the desire for maintenance of Polish traditions, for social prestige, for recreation and sociability, for political preferment and for economic improvement. Included, also, are religious interests, and a lively concern for affairs in the homeland. The total pattern constitutes a web of interrelated activities and attitudes that comprise the spiritual life of the community. Finally, inasmuch as the Polish language is used in all meetings of Polish adult groups, it is apparent that the Polish character of the community is maintained through its organized social life. (p. 174.)

Michael Parenti (1967) observed that personality considerations were also an important factor in ethnic identification, since many individuals consciously choose to associate with others of their own background. Sigmund Freud and others, however, placed greater emphasis on the unconscious forces that exercise control over the conscious thoughts and deeds of people (Hall and Lindzey, 1970). Hence, although the ethnic scale tended to produce a series of conscious attitudinal responses, it was assumed that these replies also stemmed from the use of psychological symbols that evoked the unconscious attitudes of the respondents.

A search of the literature revealed only two measures of ethnic group cohesiveness, one of which was a narrowly constructed three-point attitude scale. The items referred to the desirability of maintaining Ukrainian customs, intermarriage, and the changing of names, with any one response in an assimilationist direction defining the respondent as an assimilationist (Borhek, 1970). This research did not deal with generational and social class differences per se, and appeared to be too limited to provide for meaningful analysis of group cohesion.

The other was a more comprehensive questionnaire used to measure the ethnic identification of three generations of Japanese-Americans in Seattle. Through item analyses of a number of variables an erosion of identification was found among the generations, although a considerable residue of ethnic identity remained in the third generation. It was also observed that social mobility tended to accelerate the acculturation process. (Masuda, Matsumoto, and Meredith, 1970). The questionnaire was not adequate for the purposes of the current study, however, because it did not identify and group those religious, cultural, and national variables deemed relevant to the development of a total ethnicity construct.

CULTURAL ETHNICITY

A person's culture includes a particular set of values, beliefs, and practices, usually passed down from generation to generation and exercising a powerful influence on behavior.

There are institutions or customary practices in virtually every culture that have as their prime, if not sole, purpose association among
members of the community or some members of it. There are tribal
or community fests and festivals. There are clubs and societies, both
secret and non-secret. Groupings of this sort are, perhaps, especially
conspicuous in a culture like our own where the individual would be
lost in the vast structures of government, economics, and industry
without some small group within which he may have intimate and
personal association with his fellows. (White, 1955, pp. 9-10.)

Despite the interrelatedness of the three ethnic subscales of the current
study, the cultural construct includes key indicators of Polish-American cultural life apart from religion and nationality. The respondents were asked to
assess the importance of Polish schools, centers, organizations, and press, as
well as the perpetuation of the language, music, dance, history, and traditions
of the group.

In evaluating the cultural phenomena it is useful to recognize that the
aesthetic interests of the peasant were limited largely to popular music, poetry,
and dancing (Thomas and Znaniecki, 1918-20). Prior to World War I education
in Polonia was intended to inform the immigrant about the cultural heritage he
had never fully known and to enable him to impart it to his descendants. Hence
the growth of appreciation for the Polish literature, drama, music, and dances
of the upper class represented an attempt to create a heightened sense of
national consciousness and group pride.

Today Poles of different generations are engaged in a multiplicity of
cultural activities aimed at providing wholesome recreation, strengthening
group contact, and building self-confidence by stressing the superiority of
Polish culture (Lopata, 1964). Opera groups, dramatic societies, choirs, bands,
and dance groups have been organized to interpret the culture of Poland and to
encourage the study of the arts (Elzearia, 1954; Slesinski, 1948, Zand, 1957).

In 1948 the American Council of Polish Cultural Clubs was formed to
further the cause of cultural advancement in Polish-American communities
(Wytrwal, 1961). However, there was a dichotomy between those who fostered
programs devoted to Polish folk music, dancing, and holiday observances and
those who stressed only the classical cultural achievements, such as the music
of Chopin, as a way of presenting a better image of Polish creativity (Lopata,
1964). Despite this substantial activity, however, financial support from the
community was limited, and Polonia did not make great contributions to the
theater, the dance, or the plastic arts (Zand, 1961).

Polish patterns were also manifested in traditional foods, in the observance of holidays, and in the various practices maintained in the home. While
some of these folkways have survived, most have been modified or dropped
because of the influence of assimilationist tendencies (Zand, 1961).

The national organizations and religious institutions of Polonia were
actively involved in the effort to indoctrinate the younger generations with the
significance of their cultural traditions. The PNA funded Alliance College for

lay men and women and contributed to the maintenance of libraries and other educational centers. Institutions of higher learning were created by others, including St. Mary's College, SS. Cyril and Methodius Seminary, St. Francis College for men, Madonna College, and Immaculate Conception Junior College for women. A number of specialized educational facilities were also established, among them schools for teachers, nurses, and seminarians (Wytrwal, 1961).

A parochial school system was developed largely within the Polish Roman Catholic parishes. Large numbers of Polish-Americans attended these schools, but the numbers have steadily diminished over the years. Although they were originally designed to maintain and enrich the Polish culture, eventually there was a shift from a Polish emphasis to a curriculum resembling that of the public schools (Lopata, 1964).

Cultural interests were also stimulated by the establishment of the Kosciuszko Foundation, which is concerned with cultivating closer intellectual and cultural relations between the United States and Poland. In addition to fostering important studies in the arts and sciences it publishes the *Polish Review* and regular bulletins. The Polish American Historical Association, which publishes *Polish American Studies*, is one of a number of other groups that have been organized to encourage Polish art, culture, and history (Wytrwal, 1969).

The cultural and communal life of Polonia have also been supported by the Polish press, which provides local, national, and international news, and publicizes group activities and which has contributed to the development of an ethnic ideology. It reminds the individual of the positive aspects of Polish culture and encourages his identification with the interests of Polonia. Often, however, newspapers have tended to have particular ideological orientations, and bitter rivalries have developed among those that were proclerical or anticlerical, nationalistic and socialistic, or liberal and conservative (Olszyk, 1940).

The number of newspapers has declined substantially over the years and their influence has also diminished, especially among the young people. While sections were added in English, along with sport news, comics, and children's articles, the papers were important primarily to the older generation, whose facility in English was limited (Zand, 1957).

In 1930 there were a total of 88 Polish publications, with 84 printed in the mother tongue, 2 mixed, and 2 in English, but by 1960 this had dropped to a total of 43, with 37 in the mother tongue, 2 mixed, and 4 in English. In terms of circulation, in 1930 there were 1,037,000 Polish newspapers printed, with 999,000 in the mother tongue, 23,000 mixed, and 15,000 English. By 1960 the total had decreased to 717,000, with 690,000 in the mother tongue, 9,000 mixed, and 18,000 English (Fishman, 1966).

There was also a steady erosion in the use of the Polish language in the church, in the school, on the radio, and even in the home. Fewer schools made Polish instruction available; English rapidly supplanted Polish in the churches; and the Polish-language content of Polish radio programs was reduced appreciably. Although in 1960 a three-generation total of 2,184,936 persons claimed Polish as the mother tongue, it was employed relatively infrequently (Fishman, 1966).

It was apparent, therefore, that a number of key elements had to be taken into consideration in the construction of the cultural sub-scale. Statements were included about a wide range of Polish institutions such as schools, organizations, and the press, as well as about the importance of preserving the language, traditions, and various art forms of Polonia. These were distinguished from the religious and national items that are assessed in the following sections of this chapter.

RELIGIOUS ETHNICITY

Although the Roman Catholic church system transcends national lines in terms of its universal content, within each country it is a subsystem of the national culture. The national churches, therefore, provide an overall social structure that organizes, regulates, and helps to maintain the culture of particular ethnic groups (Warner, 1953).

Consequently there are variations among the religious practices of the different Roman Catholic nationalities in America, even though their central beliefs are essentially the same. This has provided a religio-ethnic basis for American Catholicism, linked to unique historical experiences that have made religion and ethnicity seem inseparable (Abramson and Noll, 1966; Greeley and Rossi, 1968; Marden and Meyer, 1968).

The Polish immigrant regarded his national parish in America as both a religious and a community center, a replica of his village and church in Poland and of all the activities associated with them. These included Polish schools for instruction of the young in the language, traditions, and faith as well as the spiritual, social, cultural, and welfare activities of the parish. Even more than in Poland the church became the focal point of life in Polonia, serving as a unifying factor for isolated cliques and helping to maintain the cohesion of the primary group (Swastek, 1967; Wloszczewski, 1945; Wood, 1955; Wytrwal, 1961; Zand, 1957).

> Just as the "benefit society" is much more than a mutual insurance company, so the Polish-American parish is much more than a religious association for common worship under the leadership of the priest. The unique power of the parish in Polish-American life, much greater than in even the most conservative peasant communities in Poland, cannot be explained by the predominance of religious interests which, like all other traditional social attitudes, are weakened by immigration, though they seem to be the last to disappear completely. The parish is, indeed, simply the old primary community, reorganized and concentrated. (Thomas and Znaniecki, 1918-20, Vol. 5, p. 41.)

The attitudes and feelings of parish members were embodied in stable symbols and practices, especially those of religious rites and festivals that commemorated religious and national occasions. And, while there was a strong moral-religious system, religion was interwoven with practical interests, and religious mysticism was not very developed (Madaj, 1968; Thomas and Znaniecki, 1918-20; Wood, 1955). This was apparent in the close association between religion and the Polish societies, which, with the exception of the socialistic and some professional groups, emphasized the values of Roman Catholicism as a secondary function (Lopata, 1964).

While the establishment of national parishes and parochial schools helped to facilitate the transition between Polish and American life, there were basic differences of opinion within the Church about how this was to be accomplished. Many Church leaders, particularly among the Irish-dominated hierarchy, felt that early Americanization and assimilation were essential. Others recognized the importance of helping the immigrant to adjust slowly and urged the confirmation of juridical status upon the national parishes, assuring Poles of their rights to have their own churches, served by Polish priests and following Polish customs (Maisel, 1955; Monzell, 1969).

When the Vatican refused to change its method of choosing the American episcopate, thereby confirming the Irish influence in the Church, a number of Polish parishes cut loose from Rome. As indicated in the last section of Chapter 2, they formed the Polish National Church (PNC), which still followed the Roman rite but which adopted Polish as the language of worship and established a Polish Church hierarchy (Jones, 1960; *The Polish National Catholics*, 1965). Although resentment against the Irish hierarchy continued among many of those who remained in the Roman Catholic Church, the situation improved somewhat over the years, with a number of individuals of Polish descent elevated to the episcopacy, including one who was named a Cardinal (Wytrwal, 1969).

The religious subscale of the current study is intended to measure interest in the Polish church in terms of the religious and social facets of Catholicism identified by Gerhard Lenski (1963), who concluded that religious groups were subcommunities as well as religious associations and that analysis was needed in both areas. His communal aspect was measured in terms of the degree to which the primary relations of an individual were limited to persons of his own group. The associational dimension, a type of religious orientation that transcends group lines, was measured in terms of participation in church services and activities.

For purposes of the current study it was necessary to construct a scale that deals more directly with the ethnic church, since the Lenski model was concerned with a relatively homogeneous Catholic church. The associational aspect is measured by a series of attitudinal items concerning personal feelings about participation in the Polish church as well as items concerning the importance of the church to the individual. The communal aspect is examined by using items measuring the respondent's feelings about the value of the church for others in his kin and ethnic group as well as about his personal responsibility for reaching out to them.

A critical assumption of this study is the belief that the associational and communal aspects reinforce each other in a total religio-ethnic subconstruct, particularly in light of the Polish experience, in which the church and community are unified. Because of the relative lack of mystical devotionalism and concern with church doctrine in the Polish tradition, these areas were avoided in developing the scale. It should also be noted that the Lenski model dealt with behavioral elements, while this scale is attitudinal.

NATIONAL ETHNICITY

The nineteenth century was often called "The Age of Nationalism," and saw the birth of a series of movements of national awakening, liberation, and consolidation, accompanied by a deep unrest that threatened the stability of states and the peace of the world. The fundamental tenet of these movements was that every people ought to have its own state (Wirth, 1964).

However, as indicated in the second section of Chapter 2, the Polish national consciousness had been nurtured over many centuries largely by the aristocratic and elitist groups of Polish society. Various means were developed to encourage a national loyalty, including the identification of Polish Catholicism with patriotism following the partitions that took place in the eighteenth century (Jones, 1960). But for the peasant class, which constituted the great bulk of the immigration, the discovery of national feelings was essentially a phenomenon of its American experience.

> The urbanization of many East European peoples occurred in America, not in Europe, and the effects of urbanization, its breaking down of local variation, its creation of some common denominator of nationality, its replacement of the subideological feelings of villagers with a variety of modern ideologies—these effects, all significant in making the East European peoples nations, were in large measure first displayed among them here in America (Glazer, 1954, p. 167.)

A different kind of national identification emerged that was both Polish and American, loyal to America but sensitive to the liberation of Poland from foreign oppression. The Polish-Americans emerged as a distinct and coherent group, dedicated both to the preservation of their cultural traditions and to equal participation in American life. The spirit of this adjustment process was characterized by John Barzynski, editor of the weekly *The Pilgrim*, who said:

> We shall build this type of Poland here: the Pole on American soil will never be the same as the European Pole; but, we desire that he believe as a Catholic, that he speak Polish, let him know the

traditions and history of Poland—as for the rest, let him be a Yankee. (Kruszka, 1905, pp. 107-108.)

The national subscale of the current study represents an attempt to ascertain the consequences of this bargain with America. It seeks to determine the importance of ethnic solidarity today, as well as the extent to which social intercourse with members of other groups has been inhibited. The scale items examine feelings of kinship, mutual responsibility, and a sense of belonging with others of similar background; they also touch on the sensitive nerve-endings of Polish identification, discussing Polish jokes and the propriety of Anglicizing names. This study is essentially a search for the current vitality and meaning of "peoplehood" in Polonia.

GENERATIONAL FACTORS

A number of theories have been advanced concerning the changes in ethnicity in different generations. These interrelated such factors as the length of time a group has been in America, its acceptance by those of the majority culture, and the patterns that have been developing in the increasingly mobile overall society.

It has generally been believed that the problem of a member of the second generation is that of living in two worlds; in the American environment where he is considered too foreign; and in the home of his parents where he is seen as too American. This leads to a growing gap between the generations that is often resolved by the "escape" of the child from the home of his parents.

The transition from the patriarchal, extended family system of Europe to the nuclear family pattern of America has often been highly disruptive and has led to personal disorganization, the dissolution of communal and familial solidarity, and the loss of parental influence and control. The traditions of the group have lost their hold on the individual, especially as its children became Americanized and learned to perceive the culture of their parents as inferior by the standards of the larger culture (Marden and Meyer, 1968; Thomas and Znaniecki, 1918-20; Warner, 1953).

A further consequence of this process has been the emergence of a psychological marginality among many in the second generation who are unable to adapt fully to the requirements of American culture. In seeking acceptance from the majority group and frequently finding rejection, they tend to become cultural hybrids, suffering from ambivalence, inferiority, and hyper-sensitivity. The assimilationist individual also suffers a personality conflict because of guilt feelings developed as a result of giving up his identification with his family (Green, 1947).

A significant divergence of views has emerged concerning the fear that the rejection of its heritage by the second generation would continue into the third and subsequent generations, resulting in an ultimate disappearance of the ethnic group and its traditions. As discussed in the second section of Chapter 1, some feel that there is a resurgence of ethnicity in the third generation; some see it as diminishing in a straight line; and others see it as taking new forms that hold promise for the future.

Those who believe there is a reemergence of ethnicity in the third generation feel that this group does not feel inferior because the mannerisms and possessions of its members are comparable to those of other citizens. Indeed, a great feeling of pride develops among them, leading to study of the history and culture of their ancestors.

> . . . whenever any immigrant group reaches the third-generation stage in its development a spontaneous and almost irresistible impulse arises which forces the thoughts of many people of different professions, different positions in life, and different points of view to interest themselves in that one factor which they have in common: heritage—the heritage of blood (Hansen, 1952, pp. 496-497.)

However, as noted in the second section of Chapter 1, Gans (1956) saw a more or less straight line of cultural and social assimilation in his assessment of American Jewry, with cohesiveness diminishing as Jews lose their attachment to Judaism and their minority status. This concept was also advanced by Warner (1953), who perceived assimilation in terms of the period of time a group had been in America, with mobility in the larger social system directly related to length of residence. John Thomas (1954) and Charles Marden and Gladys Meyer (1968) agreed that ethnic loyalties become less pronounced through successive generations, but Thomas also noted the maintenance of ongoing ties to the Catholic Church.

Stanley P. Wagner (1964) concluded that there is a decline in "ethnic behavior" across generations among Polish people, as measured by a decrease in correspondence with Polish relatives, subscriptions to Polish newspapers, membership in Polish clubs, and use of the Polish language. But to Niles Carpenter and Daniel Katz (1927), the second and third generations appeared to be virtually identical, while foreign-born Poles seemed to have a greater knowledge of Polish traditions than either of them.

According to Nathan Glazer (1954) and John M. Goering (1971), assimilation is not linear, and although there is a period of rejection of the past it is often followed by a return, not necessarily to the culture one has left but rather to some related but undefined ideology. This may be a reaction to such conditions of life in the United States as the problem of stereotyping, the difficulty of maintaining ethnic anonymity, and a stronger emphasis on ethnic origin in reaction to the usual stereotyping (Glazer, 1953).

Joshua A. Fishman (1966) amplified this by noting the need for a popular ideological base associated with American nationalism that could provide support for the maintenance of ethnic culture. Despite this lack, he felt that the second and subsequent generations retain and increase a marginal ethnic attachment through a growing interest in the language, even though there is no accompanying increase in usage. Wytrwal (1961) also saw a return to the study of Polish culture but believed that it has been supported by the development of an ideology in Polonia that emphasizes the importance of Polish cultural elements.

These differing views of change in ethnic cohesiveness across generations provided a background against which the research hypothesis of the current study has been developed. Although influenced by a number of diverse and interrelated elements such as the demand for cultural conformity and emerging patterns of mobility, the critical variable is seen as the length of residence in this country as measured in successive generations.

SOCIAL CLASS FACTORS

It has commonly been assumed that most young ethnics, and others of the second and third generations, have been moving to heterogeneous middle class suburbs where ethnic background tends to lose its relevance. A study of ten major cities between 1910 and 1950 by Stanley Lieberson (1962, 1963) confirmed the belief that ethnic groups become more dispersed through time. This decline in segregation was noted both among those who remained in the cities and among those who moved to the suburbs where the residents tend to be better educated and of higher socioeconomic status.

The consequences of this trend have been assessed by Scott Greer.

> At the moment, Catholics are becoming more middle class, less ethnic in culture, and suburban in residence. Social rank and suburbanization work against ethnicity, for with increasing social rank people move out of the occupational and economic worlds of kin and friends; with suburbanization they move out of the neighborhoods where they were segregated among others of "their kind." The suburbs would seem to work against preserving the ethnic subculture, for they throw the new suburbanites into relationships with neighbors of varying origins—rather than with friends, kin, paisani of the city block. (Greer, 1961, p. 624.)

Warner and Leo Srole (1945) and Warner (1953) supported the belief that the social class system of America permitted an upward mobility that could be highly disruptive to the ethnic group. As members of the younger generation identified with the culture of the larger society they frequently repudiated the standards and values of the older generation, and the hold of the traditional family was diminished or destroyed. Also, as educational and economic opportunities increased, the life style and social status of many tended to change radically, with a resultant upward drift in social rank.

But although ethnic segregation weakened, the reports of its demise were exaggerated. In recent years a number of observers have suggested that there are enclaves even in suburban areas and that ethnic interests and identity are still being expressed in different ways (Graham and Gurr, 1969; Parenti, 1967).

Further, Etzioni (1959) indicated that residential segregation is not a necessary prerequisite for the maintenance of ethnic subgroups, and that there is a third, long-range alternative to segregation and assimilation. He described the emergence of a middle group that has found a new way of maintaining its identity and cohesion in a diverse society. It is marked by a transition from the enclave membership group of the city to the suburban reference group, which is maintained by communication, limited social situations, and core institutions.

Ethnic continuity in the new environment is also the result of the maintenance of marks of social superiority and rejection that distinguish the dominant and minority groups in America. Many a person can do something about his economic situation and yet be powerless with respect to his ethnic background unless he denies it. Consequently, upward social mobility and assimilation are often thwarted, and group solidarity is heightened by the attitudes of the core group that identifies the ethnics as undesirable (Cole and Cole, 1954; Hollingshead and Redlich, 1958).

The fluid nature of socioeconomic conditions in America made it necessary to construct a typology of socioeconomic status (SES) relevant to the current condition of ethnic groups in general and Polish-Americans in particular. Herbert Gans (1962) and August B. Hollingshead and Frederick C. Redlich (1958) agreed that there are a number of different ways in which class can be defined, depending on the orientation of the researcher. Some looked at shared characteristics such as group interests and social relationships; some were concerned mainly with occupation, on the assumption that work determines access to income, power, and status, thereby influencing behavior; and others focused on an aggregate of characteristics such as education, income, occupation, and residence.

While taking such criteria into account, Gans felt that it could be misleading to stress any single factor. Hence he defined the various social class groupings as subcultures and identified them in terms of behavior patterns, attitudes, and life styles.

According to Gans, the lower-class subculture is distinguished by the female-based family and the marginal male, with the woman seeking stability in the midst of poverty and the man living an unpredictable, episodic life. The working class tends to be detached from the larger society and is concerned largely with the family circle and peer group relations rather than object-goals.

The middle class subculture, however, is oriented more toward economic growth and status considerations, with education seen as a vehicle for advancement. It is also built around the nuclear family and its desire to make its way in the larger society. Thus it differs from the working class, which places a higher value on family and personal friendship as opposed to material success.

The professional upper-middle-class culture is also organized around the nuclear family, but it places greater emphasis than does the middle class on maximizing the development of its individual members. Hence, work is not seen primarily in terms of family needs and economic gain but as an opportunity for personal achievement and satisfaction.

Movement from one class to another is viewed as a slow process of culture change that may take a generation or more and that results from new opportunities and a willingness to accept them. Since many people are in transition from one subculture to another, however, there are difficulties in categorizing them according to the Gans typology.

Hollingshead's Index of Social Position is premised on three assumptions that make it easier to categorize the class subcultures: (1) that social stratification exists in the community, (2) that status positions are determined mainly by a few commonly accepted cultural characteristics, and (3) that items symbolic of status may be combined to stratify the population.

Place of residence, education, and occupation are the key elements of the Index; this is based on the belief that a family's mode of living is mirrored in its home, that the occupation of its head denotes its members' influence in society, and that the amount of his formal education reflects the tastes of his family.

For the purposes of the current study a social class typology has been constructed utilizing the principles that are the basis of the Hollingshead Index, but expanding the number of indicators to include income and type of automobile owned. Gans' four social class categories are included, with his "professional upper-middle class" identified in this study as the "upper class." Consequently, upper-class status as it is understood in this study is not comparable to that of the upper class in the general population, where it is based largely on family position and prestige (Baltzell, 1964).

SUMMARY

Through the construction of a group cohesiveness scale, an ethnic identity model has been developed that employs religious, cultural, and national variables. The model emphasizes the interrelatedness of these subconstructs, which together constitute a total measure of ethnicity. The generational and social-class variables are then assessed in terms of their relationship to ethnic continuity. The model was tested with the hypothesis that ethnic identification is diminishing as factors of cultural conformity and social mobility reduce the holding power of ethnic groups over time.

4

METHODOLOGY

This chapter sets forth the methodology employed in the study, including the research design, the procedure, the sample, the dependent and independent variables, the testable hypotheses, and the statistical tests, as they relate to the research question and area of study.

THE RESEARCH DESIGN

The research design selected to investigate the research question and area of study is ex post facto in nature (Kerlinger, 1964): the subjects have self-selected themselves as a Polish-American group with varying degrees of ethnic cohesiveness.

In the ex post facto research approach, the independent variables are examined in an effort to explain the presumed differences in ethnicity. The ex post facto design assumes that the independent variables have already occurred and cannot be manipulated, but that they can be interpreted. Hence, after the dependent variables of ethnicity are observed, the independent variables of generation and social class are studied in retrospect in order to note their effect on or relation to ethnicity.

THE DATA-GATHERING PROCEDURE

For the reasons given in Chapter 3, the gathering of data necessitated the development of an ethnicity scale and questionnaire. Following a search of the literature and consultation with authoritative individuals, a total ethnicity scale was developed with cultural, religious, and national subconstructs.

Correspondence was also initiated with the Polish American Historical Association, Congressman Roman Pucinski, the Library of Congress, and researchers working in related areas. In addition, contact was made with a number of other Polish-American groups and leaders in order to identify the symbolic elements and facets of life in Polonia that would have special meaning in the scale.

The scale was validated by a broadly representative panel of twenty experts from a number of university faculties across the country, including persons knowledgeable in the social sciences and ethnic research. A total of 75 items was presented to the judges, who were asked to indicate on an 11 point scale the value of each item for the measurement of religious, cultural, and national ethnic cohesiveness.

The responses of the panel were tabulated and the 10 most valid items from each of the subconstructs were included in the scale, with the total of 30 items to be considered a measure of ethnicity. Special care was taken to divide the items of the religious subscale equally between the associational and communal aspects of religion identified by Lenski and adapted for the current study as indicated in the fourth section of Chapter 3.

This study encountered initial, and in some cases continuing, resistance by some officials of Polish-American groups, who apparently felt considerable suspicion about the motivation behind the research project. Although letters were secured from the faculty of the University of Southern California (USC) to assure these persons of the legitimacy of the investigation, resistance continued for a considerable time and in some cases was never overcome. Subsequently, however, Antoinette Rydzeski, an officer of the Polish American Congress, assisted greatly by securing the help of a number of people who participated in the construction of the scale, in the pilot study, and in the interviewing process itself.

One male and three female interviewers were selected and trained to assist in the data gathering process. They were attractive, college-age people who, it was felt, would be likely to gain the confidence of those to be interviewed. Because a language problem was anticipated with some of the foreign-born respondents, one of the interviewers chosen was a young woman with facility in the Polish language.

The interviewers were asked to request private interviews, to keep the responses from being influenced by the presence of others. They were urged to conduct the interviews in a helpful, friendly, but impersonal manner to avoid biasing the results. The interviewers themselves were asked to fill out the self-administered questionnaires as part of their training, to help them deal with problems of understanding that might arise.

In preparing the interviewers for their task, particular emphasis was placed on enabling them to deal tactfully with the anticipated anxieties and concerns of those to be interviewed, as the Polish-American group seems to be, for the most part, unaccustomed to being asked personal questions. Earlier discussions with members of the community, as well as the pilot study, had indicated strong feelings for privacy. (The pilot study is described in the fourth section of this chapter.) It was vital, therefore, to assure the respondents that their confidentiality would be respected and anonymity preserved.

It was also felt that the length of the interview process could be a problem, since the pilot study revealed that it could take from thirty minutes to two hours, depending on the ability of the respondents to deal with the questions. This was emphasized by some of the ethnic experts, who believed the subjects would not submit to a long interview. Consequently the skill of the interviewers in relating to the respondents was especially important.

Some of those to be interviewed received a letter from Antoinette Rydze-ski that explained the purpose of the study in general terms and contained a request for cooperation. Follow-up telephone calls were made by the interviewers to set up mutually convenient appointments. A letter of introduction from a USC faculty member was provided to each of the interviewers to show that the research project was legitimate.

THE SAMPLING PROCEDURE

A stratified-purposive sampling procedure was used to select a sample that would be broadly representative. An effort was made to find people who would provide a cross-section of the Polish-American community in the Los Angeles Metropolitan Area.

As a result of the wide distribution of the population randomization was not possible, but every effort was made to overcome the problem of self-selection. In the sample were persons of all generations and classes, including those affiliated and not affiliated with Polish organizations and some who were seeking to avoid contact with Polish life. A balance was sought that took into account differences of age, sex, generation, income, religious affiliation, community involvement, marital status, and other socioeconomic factors. Contacts in the Polish and general communities assisted in an intensive search for a matched sample.

In addition to working-class young people not attending college, a special effort was made to look for respondents among those of the third and fourth generations, eighteen years of age or older, on three Catholic college campuses in the area. Priests of Polish descent on two of the faculties reviewed the student rosters, identifying some by names that they believed to be Polish and pointing out others whom they knew to be Polish regardless of their names.

Some 50 percent of those identified by the priests as having Polish names said that they were not of Polish ancestry. Although a similarity in some Slavic names makes for a strong possibility of error in name identification, but since there were so many it is likely that some of the students may have been unwilling to acknowledge their Polish heritage.

Of the 126 persons selected for the total sample, there were nine refusals, five individuals who could not be reached, and one uncompleted questionnaire, leaving a total of 111 completed interviews. Among the reasons given for the refusals were problems of health, lack of time, and dislike for the research project.

THE PILOT STUDY

This scale and an accompanying questionnaire for collecting other data were used in a pilot study in the fall of 1970, with a sample consisting of twelve individuals representing widely divergent backgrounds. As a consequence of this process the scale and questionnaire were changed a number of times to facilitate comprehension and to improve on the content in terms of the research objectives.

The methodology described in this chapter was utilized in the pilot study, but the pilot study itself was part of the methodological approach and contributed to it in an evolving process of change. It was especially useful in evaluating the feasibility and relevance of the research design, and particularly the viability of the ethnicity scale as a vehicle for obtaining meaningful empirical differences.

THE DEPENDENT VARIABLES

As indicated earlier, the measurement of the ethnicity variables is a crucial element of the research design. Since Allen L. Edwards (1957) and others had noted that many people are reluctant to share their feelings about sensitive personal matters, it was felt that direct questioning on ethnic attitudes would be of limited value.

Since no suitable instrument was available a scale was constructed for the measurement of attitudes that included a number of psychological objects. L. L. Thurstone (1928) defined an "attitude" as the degree of positive or negative effect associated with some psychological object. He described as a psychological object any symbol, phrase, idea, or institution toward which people can express positive or negative responses.

Consequently, a number of items were selected that, it was believed, represented the universe of interest and toward which the interviewee might express varying degrees of positive or negative response. Particular care was taken to observe the criteria summarized by Edwards pertaining to the construction of attitude scales, including avoidance of statements that can be interpreted in more than one way or that are likely to be endorsed by everyone or no one. It is also essential to develop statements that are short, direct, and clear.

A number of the items were put in the negative form and later reversed in the coding process. The three subconstructs were mixed together to make the scale appear to the respondent as a unified entity.

This is a summated rating scale, also known as a Likert-type scale, consisting of a number of items of approximately equal value (Murphy and Likert, 1937). A six-point scale was employed, ranging from "strongly agree" to "strongly disagree." After the subjects responded to the statements with varying degrees of agreement or disagreement, the scores were summed and averaged to yield an individual's attitude score.

This made it possible to place the respondent on an agreement continuum that yielded interval-level data. Hence, the dependent variables of this study were measured in terms of mean levels of response to the religious, cultural, and national subscales, as well as to the total ethnicity construct.

THE INDEPENDENT VARIABLES

The independent variables were separated according to generational and social-class differences.

The seven generational variables were divided in terms of foreign or American birth, arrival in this country before or after World War II, and generation of nativity in the United States. These were nominal data that were countable and classifiable. The generational variables are shown in Table 4.1.

A social class construct was developed for the current study, recognizing that a number of different groupings is possible according to the judgment of

TABLE 4.1

Generational Variables

Number of Category	Description of Variable
1	First generation foreign-born who came to the United States before World War II
2	First generation foreign-born who came to the United States during or after World War II
3	Second generation American-born
4	Third generation American-born
5	Fourth generation American-born
6	All of the American-born
7	All of the foreign-born

TABLE 4.2

Social Class Variables

Social Class	Weekly Family Income (1)	Education (2)	Occupation (3)	Type of Car (4)	Home Ownership (5)
Upper class	300 and up	Graduate, 6 years of college	Professional	1969-71 luxury	Own home
Middle class	200-299	Graduate, 4 years of college	Businessman	1969-71 moderate	Own home
Working class	100-199	High school graduate	White collar or blue collar, skilled or semi-skilled	1966 or older	Do not own home
Lower class	Under 100	Less than high school	Blue collar, unskilled	No car	Do not own home

the researcher. The construct was based on a number of key variables including family income, education, occupation, make of car, and home ownership. As illustrated in Table 4.2, social class was assigned through the identification of an individual with two out of three of items 1 to 3, plus one out of two of items 4 and 5. The social class positions were nominal data that were countable and classifiable.

The process was initiated by relating the respondent to the upper-class category and moving successively to other positions until the correct grouping was found. Personal judgment was used at times in making the final determination, especially in marginal cases.

The data on occupation were gathered and tabulated in nine categories as illustrated in Table 4.3. These were regrouped for the designated social classes as shown in Table 4.2. For housewives, the retired, the unemployed, and students, the decision on social class was based on identification with two out of two from columns 1 and 2 and one out of two from columns 4 and 5. This was considered appropriate since social class status could thus be related to family income and family home ownership.

THE STATISTICAL TECHNIQUES

The research question established in Chapter 1 proposes investigation of any differences in ethnic cohesiveness that might occur between the seven generational and four social class variables described in the previous section.

TABLE 4.3

Occupational Variables

Number of Category	Type of Occupation
1	Professional
2	Managerial, entrepreneurial
3	Clerical, sales, white-collar
4	Blue-collar: skilled, semi-skilled
5	Blue-collar: unskilled
6	Housewife
7	Retired
8	Unemployed
9	Student

For these inferential analyses, student's t tests were employed to examine the probable tenability of the null hypotheses. These tests help to assess the significance of the difference between two sample means.

According to Hubert M. Blalock (1960), the practical value of the t test is in situations where there are small samples and where a normal population can be assumed. This inductive statistic can be used in making generalizations or drawing inferences about relations or differences between the generational and social class variables.

The basic descriptive statistics utilized included frequencies, percentages, means, and standard deviations. Both the descriptive and inferential statistics are presented in tables in Chapter 5.

CODING AND PROCESSING THE DATA

A coded abbreviation was assigned to each of the variables to facilitate handling of the data in the electronic data-processing medium. Table 4.4 presents these coded abbreviations as they will appear in the data tables.

TABLE 4.4

Abbreviated Names of Variables

Abbreviated Name	Description of Variable
FB PRE 2	First generation foreign-born who came to the United States before World War II
FB POS 2	First generation foreign-born who came to the United States during or after World War II
2 GEN AB	Second generation American-born
3 GEN AB	Third generation American-born
4 GEN AB	Fourth generation American-born
ALL FOR	All of the foreign-born
ALL AME	All of the American-born
UP CLAS	Upper-class
MI CLAS	Middle-class
WK CLAS	Working-class
LO CLAS	Lower-class

The data were punched into data processing cards and processed at the University of Southern California Computer Services Laboratory. The programs were set up for use with an IBM System 360 computer.

SUMMARY

This chapter has presented the methodology employed in the current study, including the ex post facto research design, the procedure used for gathering the data, the method of sampling, operational definitions of the dependent and independent variables, and an assessment of the statistical tests as they pertain to the research question. The following chapter will deal with a presentation of the descriptive and inferential data related to this area of study.

CHAPTER

5

PRESENTATION
OF THE DATA

This chapter presents the results of the data analyses and explores the research question by examining the tenability of the null hypotheses. Both descriptive and inferential data will be shown in sections pertaining to the generational and social-class groupings. Additional tables of descriptive data are included in the appendix, to aid in the assessment of basic data characteristics.

ANALYSIS OF THE GENERATIONAL GROUPS

In examining Null Hypothesis A, which is given in the fifth section of Chapter 1, the students' t tests were computed to determine whether any significant differences could be observed between the various generational groupings. To facilitate analysis of the "straight line" theory of the loss of ethnic cohesiveness, the seven generational variables were divided into two Matrixes, one dealing with differences between the five generational groups and the other organizing them into all-American and all-foreign categories.

The descriptive data for the five generational groups are offered in Tables 5.1 through 5.6, while the inferential data for these groups are presented separately in Tables 5.7 through 5.12, according to the dependent variables of ethnicity. Additional descriptive and inferential data for the all-American and all-foreign categories are combined in Table 5.13.

Some of the percentages in the tables of descriptive data are presented in a number of columns, which together total 100 percent. An example is Table 5.1, where the items in the first and second columns are combined for a total of 100 percent. Particular attention should also be given to the inclusion of the all-foreign and all-American categories, which represent separate entities and are not part of the totals indicated above.

TABLE 5.1

Generational Groups Categorized by Sex

Generational Group	Male		Female	
	Number of Respondents	Percent	Number of Respondents	Percent
FB PRE 2	4	3.6	10	9.0
FB POS 2	12	10.8	8	7.2
2 GEN AB	17	15.3	26	23.4
3 GEN AB	11	9.9	12	10.8
4 GEN AB	9	8.1	2	1.8
ALL FOR	16	14.4	18	16.2
ALL AME	37	33.3	40	36.0
Total	53	47.7	58	52.3

Source: Compiled by the author.

A profile of the sample used in the current study emerges through an analysis of the descriptive data presented in Tables 5.1 through 5.6. Table 5.1 indicates that 47.7 percent of the total sample of 111 persons were male and 52.3 percent were female. As might be expected, there were fewer males among those in the pre-World War II category because the longevity of females is greater than that of males. The small number of females in the fourth generation was the result of an inability to locate more of this group in the Los Angeles area.

As indicated in Table 5.2, the marital status of the sample suggests a very stable group, with only 2.7 percent having been divorced and none separated. Of the total sample, 64.8 percent were married, 26.1 percent were single, and 6.3 percent were widowed.

The educational level of the sample is shown in Table 5.3 and points to the fact that 29.7 percent have a college or graduate diploma. This high degree of education is particularly evident among the foreign-born who came to the United States after World War II. Of this group, 40 percent are college-educated or better, while none of the foreign-born who came to America before World War II has more than a high school diploma.

Analysis of the groups indicates an increasing measure of attainment in succeeding generations, from the relatively uneducated foreign-born who came before World War II through the second and the third generations born in the United States. The data for the fourth generation do not support this trend because a number of younger people are included who have not yet had an

TABLE 5.2

Generational Groups Categorized by Marital Status

Generational Group	Married		Divorced		Widowed		Single	
	Number of Respondents	Percent	Number of Respondents	Percent	Number of Respondents	Percent	Number of Respondents	Percent
FB PRE 2	8	7.2	1	0.9	5	4.5	—	—
FB POS 2	15	13.5	—	—	—	—	5	4.5
2 GEN AB	37	33.3	1	0.9	2	1.8	3	2.7
3 GEN AB	11	9.9	—	—	—	—	12	10.8
4 GEN AB	1	0.9	1	0.9	—	—	9	8.1
ALL FOR	23	20.7	1	0.9	5	4.5	5	4.5
ALL AME	49	44.1	2	1.8	2	1.8	24	21.6
Total	72	64.8	3	2.7	7	6.3	29	26.1

Note: There were no respondents in the "Separated" category.
Source: Compiled by the author.

TABLE 5.3

Generational Groups Categorized by Education

Generational Group	Less than High School Graduate		High School Graduate		College Graduate		6 Years of College	
	Number of Respondents	Percent	Number of Respondents	Percent	Number of Respondents	Percent	Number of Respondents	Percent
FB PRE 2	8	7.2	6	5.4				
FB POS 2	1	0.9	11	9.9	4	3.6	4	3.6
2 GEN AB	11	9.9	20	18.0	9	8.1	3	2.7
3 GEN AB			14	12.6	6	5.4	3	2.7
4 GEN AB			7	6.3	3	2.7	1	0.9
ALL FOR	9	8.1	17	15.3	4	3.6	4	3.6
ALL AME	11	9.9	41	36.9	18	16.2	7	6.3
Total	20	18.0	58	52.2	22	19.8	11	9.9

Source: Compiled by the author.

opportunity to complete their schooling. However, the educational level of the fourth generation is presently comparable to that of the third.

It should be noted that, despite the upward educational mobility of Polish-Americans generationally, the great majority have a limited education. This is underscored by the fact that 70.2 percent have not received a college degree. As indicated earlier, however, the amount of formal training of Polish-Americans in the Los Angeles area may be greater than that of the population in the Eastern enclaves of Polonia.

Tables 5.4 to 5.6 offer insights into the religious practices of the sample. The predominance of the Roman Catholic Church is shown in all categories; only a small percentage is identified in other ways. The figures indicate that Roman Catholics are 89.2 percent of the total; Polish National Catholics, 2.7 percent; Protestants, 4.5 percent; and "no designation," 3.6 percent.

There are, however, important differences in religious habits as identified in Table 5.5, with membership in the Polish churches showing a consistent decline according to generation. Figures of 85 percent and 78.6 percent are reported in the post- and pre-World War II groups respectively. These are reduced to 46.5 percent in the second generation, 21.7 percent in the third, and 9.1 percent in the fourth.

At the same time, membership in non-Polish churches remains consistently high, increasing from 71.4 percent among the pre-World War II foreign-born to 72.1 percent in the second generation and 78.3 percent in the third. A sharp decrease in church membership in the fourth generation is indicated by the drop to 54.5 percent.

The data in Table 5.6 also point to changes in religious behavior, with Polish church attendance declining in the third and fourth generations. However, attendance at services of the non-Polish churches remains fairly constant until the fourth generation, where it, too, declines.

The loss of ethnic cohesiveness over generations is suggested by the data in Table 5.7. Mean levels of ethnicity decline generationally in all categories of the ethnic scale, with higher scores corresponding to decreased commitment.

While the religious and national ethnicity scores diminish over generations, the cultural ethnicity pattern is less consistent, with the foreign-born and the second generation approximately the same. However, the level of cultural ethnicity is reduced successively from the second to the third and fourth generations.

The total ethnicity construct shows a consistent but irregular reduction, with mean levels of ethnicity going from 73.79 and 67.25 in the pre- and post-World War II groups respectively to 80.88 in the second generation, 105.57 in the third, and 116.09 in the fourth.

Despite the decrease in mean levels of ethnic cohesiveness in virtually all generational categories, an examination of Null Hypothesis A indicates that only some of the differences are significant at the .05 or .01 levels. Tables 5.8 through 5.12 present the results of the analysis of Null Hypothesis A.

It may be observed from these four tables that the null hypothesis of no difference between means of total and national ethnicity scale scores may be

TABLE 5.4

Generational Groups Categorized by Religion

Generational Group	Roman Catholic		Polish National Catholic		Protestant		None	
	Number of Respondents	Percent	Number of Respondents	Percent	Number of Respondents	Percent	Number of Respondents	Percent
FB PRE 2	13	11.7	—	—	1	0.9	—	—
FB POS 2	19	17.1	1	0.9	—	—	—	—
2 GEN AB	39	35.1	1	0.9	2	1.8	1	0.9
3 GEN AB	20	18.0	—	—	1	0.9	2	1.8
4 GEN AB	8	7.2	1	0.9	1	0.9	1	0.9
ALL FOR	32	28.8	1	0.9	1	0.9	—	—
ALL AME	67	60.4	2	1.8	4	3.6	4	3.6
Total	99	89.2	3	2.7	5	4.5	4	3.6

Source: Compiled by the author.

51

TABLE 5.5

Generational Groups Categorized by Membership in Polish and Non-Polish Churches

Generational Group	Total Number of Respondents	Polish Church			Non-Polish Church		
		Number of Members*	Percent of Generational Sample	Percent of Total Sample	Number of Members*	Percent of Generational Sample	Percent of Total Sample
FB PRE 2	14	11	78.6	9.9	10	71.4	9.0
FB POS 2	20	17	85.0	15.3	13	65.0	11.7
2 GEN AB	43	20	46.5	18.0	31	72.1	27.9
3 GEN AB	23	5	21.7	4.5	18	78.3	16.2
4 GEN AB	11	1	9.1	0.9	6	54.5	5.4
ALL FOR	34	28	82.4	25.2	23	67.7	20.7
ALL AME	77	26	33.4	23.4	55	71.4	49.5
Total	111	54	—	48.6	78	—	70.2

*Some respondents were members of both churches.
Source: Compiled by the author.

TABLE 5.6

Generational Groups Categorized by Attendance
at Polish and Non-Polish Church Services

Generational Group	Mean Level of Attendance at Polish Services per Year	Mean Level of Attendance at Non-Polish Services per Month
FB PRE 2	11.93	2.93
FB POS 2	22.20	3.55
2 GEN AB	12.53	3.09
3 GEN AB	1.83	3.39
4 GEN AB	4.55	1.82

Source: Compiled by the author.

rejected at the .01 level of significance for the tests between the post-World War II foreign-born and the second generation American-born as well as between the second and third generation American-born. Hence, the research hypothesis of significant difference may be accepted with the assurance that the probability of making an error in this decision is less than one percent.

Table 5.9 shows that the hypothesis of no difference between mean levels of religious ethnicity of the foreign-born of post-World War II and the second generation is untenable at the .05 level, while it is untenable at the .01 level between the second and third generations. As shown in Table 5.11, no significant difference in cultural ethnicity was found between the post-world War II group and the second generation, but the difference between the second and third generations was significant at the .01 level.

In all of the ethnic scale categories the null hypotheses of no difference are tenable between the third and fourth generations. The null hypotheses are also tenable between the pre- and post-World War II foreign-born except for national ethnicity, which is untenable at the .05 level. Also, when the foreign-born groups are combined as shown in Table 5.12 the null hypotheses of no difference between the foreign-born and second generation are untenable in all categories and are rejected at the .05 level, with a 5 percent probability of error in accepting the research hypothesis. The exception is cultural ethnicity, where the difference in means is not significant.

When all of the foreign-born are compared to all of the American-born, as shown in Table 5.13, a clear pattern of difference emerges, with null hypotheses found strongly untenable at the .01 level of significance or better. Hence, the research hypotheses may be accepted with the probability of Alpha error at one percent.

TABLE 5.7

Means and Standard Deviations of Ethnicity Scale Scores for Generational Groups

Generational Group	Number of Respondents	Ethnicity Scale Scores							
		Religious Ethnicity		National Ethnicity		Cultural Ethnicity		Total Ethnicity	
		Mean	Standard Deviation	Mean	Standard Deviation	Mean	Standard Deviation	Mean	Standard Deviation
FB PRE 2	14	25.71	8.31	28.43	8.79	20.79	7.46	73.79	19.47
FB POS 2	20	25.30	7.77	22.40	5.29	19.55	4.88	67.25	13.98
2 GEN AB	43	30.12	10.87	31.00	8.28	20.70	8.88	80.88	23.95
3 GEN AB	23	39.13	8.75	38.22	7.20	28.65	7.19	105.57	22.22
4 GEN AB	11	43.27	10.70	39.09	8.96	33.73	10.89	116.09	27.58

Source: Compiled by the author.

TABLE 5.8

Significant t Ratios for Differences between Means of Total Ethnicity Scale Scores for Generational Groups

Generational Groups	Generational Groups Compared			
	FB POS 2	2 GEN AB	3 GEN AB	4 GEN AB
FB PRE 2	n.s.	n.s.	4.54[a]	4.27[a]
FB POS 2	—	2.90[a]	6.84[a]	5.48[a]
2 GEN AB	—	—	4.26[a]	3.87[a]
3 GEN AB	—	—	—	n.s.

n.s. = not significant
[a]$p. < .01$
Source: Compiled by the author.

TABLE 5.9

Significant t Ratios for Differences between Means of Religious Ethnicity Scale Scores for Generational Groups

Generational Groups	Generational Groups Compared			
	FB POS 2	2 GEN AB	3 GEN AB	4 GEN AB
FB PRE 2	n.s.	n.s.	4.78[b]	4.51[b]
FB POS 2	—	2.01[a]	5.52[b]	5.00[b]
2 GEN AB	—	—	3.60[b]	3.67[b]
3 GEN AB	—	—	—	n.s.

n.s. = not significant
[a]$p. < .05$
[b]$p. < .01$
Source: Compiled by the author.

ANALYSIS OF THE SOCIAL CLASS GROUPS

Analysis of the data in Table 5.14 shows that mean levels of ethnic cohesiveness are virtually the same in the upper- and middle-class groups. This suggests that the two samples are representative of the same population. Clear differences are evident, however, between the upper and working classes as well as between the middle and working classes.

Null Hypothesis B is examined through Tables 5.15 to 5.18, in which data are presented on significant t ratios for differences between means of social

TABLE 5.10

Significant t Ratios for Differences between Means of National Ethnicity Scale Scores for Generational Groups

Generational Groups	Generational Groups Compared			
	FB POS 2	2 GEN AB	3 GEN AB	4 GEN AB
FB PRE 2	2.56^a	n.s.	3.50^b	2.94^b
FB POS 2	—	4.77^b	8.32^b	5.76^b
2 GEN AB	—	—	3.60^b	2.70^b
3 GEN AB	—	—	—	n.s.

n.s. = not significant
[a]p. <.05
[b]p. <.01
Source: Compiled by the author.

TABLE 5.11

Significant t Ratios for Differences between Means of Cultural Ethnicity Scale Scores for Generational Groups

Generational Groups	Generational Groups Compared			
	FB POS 2	2 GEN AB	3 GEN AB	4 GEN AB
FB PRE 2	n.s.	n.s.	3.04^a	3.33^a
FB POS 2	—	n.s.	4.79^a	4.06^a
2 GEN AB	—	—	3.96^a	3.71^a
3 GEN AB	—	—	—	n.s.

n.s. = not significant
[a]p. <.01
Source: Compiled by the author.

class groups. These are shown according to the four scale categories of religious, national, cultural, and total ethnicity.

As indicated previously, no significant differences were found between the upper and middle classes, but differences between the middle and working classes were found to be significant at the .01 level in all categories with the probability of Alpha error at one percent. An exception was religious ethnicity, which was significant at the .05 level.

TABLE 5.12

Significant t Ratios for Differences between Means of Total Ethnicity Scale Scores for All of the Foreign-born and for the Second-Generation American-born

Ethnicity Scales	t Ratios between 2 GEN AB (N = 43) and ALL FOR (N = 34)
Total ethnicity	t = 2.43, p. <.05
Religious ethnicity	t = 2.25, p. <.05
National ethnicity	t = 3.48, p. <.05
Cultural ethnicity	n.s.

Source: Compiled by the author.

TABLE 5.13

Means and Standard Deviations of Ethnicity Scale Scores for Foreign-born versus American-born Polish-Americans

Ethnicity Scales	Foreign-born (N = 34)		American-born (N = 77)		t Ratio
	Mean	Standard Deviation	Mean	Standard Deviation	
Religious	25.47	7.87	34.69	11.44	t = 5.11, p. <.01
National	24.88	7.46	34.31	8.81	t = 3.48, p. <.01
Cultural	20.06	6.00	24.94	9.98	t = 3.27, p. <.01
Total	69.94	16.51	93.29	27.71	t = 5.55, p. <.01

Source: Compiled by the author.

TABLE 5.14

Means and Standard Deviations of Ethnicity Scale Scores for Social Class Groups

Social Class Groups	Number of Respondents	Ethnicity Scale Scores							
		Religious Ethnicity		National Ethnicity		Cultural Ethnicity		Total Ethnicity	
		Mean	Standard Deviation	Mean	Standard Deviation	Mean	Standard Deviation	Mean	Standard Deviation
UP CLAS	17	34.65	11.56	33.06	10.49	25.12	12.71	92.82	30.08
MI CLAS	47	33.91	12.07	34.51	9.84	25.43	9.44	93.09	28.89
WK CLAS	47	28.81	9.77	27.74	7.35	20.85	6.76	77.40	21.42

Note: There were no respondents in the Lower Class category.
Source: Compiled by the author.

TABLE 5.15

Significant t Ratios for Differences between Means of Total Ethnicity Scale Scores for Social Class Groups

Social Class Groups	Social Class Groups Compared	
	MI CLAS	WK CLAS
UP CLAS	n.s.	1.61^a
MI CLAS	—	3.02^b

n.s. = not significant
^{a}p. <.10
^{b}p. <.01
Source: Compiled by the author.

Null Hypothesis B for the upper- and working-class groups was found untenable at the .10 level in all categories except cultural ethnicity, where it was tenable even at this weak level. This may be explained by the differences in sample sizes, since the number of respondents from the middle class, helps to achieve significance more readily than does the number of upper class respondents, which was 17.

Null Hypothesis B, which says that ethnicity does not vary inversely with social class, is therefore rejected in part. The working class is significantly more ethnic than either the middle or the upper classes, but these latter two groupings are not appreciably different.

TABLE 5.16

Significant t Ratios for Differences between Means of Religious Ethnicity Scale Scores for Social Class Groups

Social Class Groups	Social Class Groups Compared	
	MI CLAS	WK CLAS
UP CLAS	n.s.	1.85^a
MI CLAS	—	2.32^b

n.s. = not significant
^{a}p. <.10
^{b}p. <.05
Source: Compiled by the author.

TABLE 5.17

Significant t Ratios for Differences between Means of National
Ethnicity Scale Scores for Social Class Groups

Social Class	Social Class Groups Compared	
Groups	MI CLAS	WK CLAS
UP CLAS	n.s.	1.89[a]
MI CLAS	—	3.77[b]

n.s. = not significant
[a]p. <.10
[b]p. <.01
Source: Compiled by the author.

ANALYSIS OF THE GROUP COHESIVENESS SCALE

The group cohesiveness scale and an analysis of the individual measures in terms of mean levels of ethnic identification by social class and generational groups are presented in Figure 5.1 and Tables 5.19 and 5.20.

The working class gave more ethnic responses than the middle or upper classes to 26 of the 30 scale items in Figure 5.1. The items where the middle or upper classes responded more strongly ethnically have to do with attitudes

TABLE 5.18

Significant t Ratios for Differences between Means of Cultural
Ethnicity Scale Scores for Social Class Groups

Social Class	Social Class Groups Compared	
Groups	MI CLAS	WK CLAS
UP CLAS	n.s.	n.s.
MI CLAS	—	2.71[a]

n.s. = not significant
[a]p. <.01
Source: Compiled by the author.

about helping others (20, 29), the need for cultural centers (14), and religious education for the young (6). However, these may be more of an indication of the humanitarian and educational concerns of the upwardly mobile than a reflection of ethnic consciousness. Further, the differences among the responses to these items according to social class are small.

In responding to the very personal religious associational items (2, 11, 15, 17, 25), working class ethnics agreed that they feel more comfortable in a Polish church, especially at Christmas; that they prefer services in the Polish language; that the Polish religious tradition strengthens family life; and that they are willing to travel to the Polish church even if it is far from home. This is somewhat different from the responses of the upper and middle classes, which shaded toward disagreement on these matters—except about the Polish Christmas Mass, which struck a responsive chord in all.

As for the religious communal items that reflect attitudes toward the behavior of others (6, 8, 19, 23, 29), all are in mild agreement that families should be encouraged to belong to (23) and attend (8) the Polish church; that the Polish religious education is important(6); and that there is an obligation to help new people in the Polish parish get settled (29). It is only the working class, however, that is willing to contribute its time, talent, and finances to the Polish church (19).

There is significant agreement among all social class groups that Polish culture is important and should be strengthened. Approval is shown toward teaching about the contribution of Poles to America (1), toward organizations which carry on the Polish culture (5, 14), toward Polish dance and music (7, 24), toward a Polish newspaper (10), and toward knowing the Polish language, history (28, 16), and tradition (21, 26). In all of these areas, with the exception of their responses to the item about supporting cultural centers for the young (14), the working class expressed much more ethnic cultural identification.

A sense of peoplehood is emphasized in the national ethnicity subscale through support on the part of all classes, but especially the working class, of such beliefs as that a feeling for the Polish people is "in the blood" (9); that Poles can count on one another for help (20); and that it is better to marry someone of the same nationality (22). This is reinforced by the belief that one can be a good American despite a prior loyalty to the primary group (30).

Differences are found among the social classes with respect to other national items. The working class showed a tendency to feel more comfortable with Polish people (13), especially in a Polish neighborhood (4). The ethnic identity of the working class is also evident in its rejection of name changing (12) and greater concern with Polish jokes (18). All groups were unwilling to use Polish nationality as a criterion in selecting a political candidate (27), but the working class was more ready to do this than the others were.

In the responses to 20 of the 30 scale items there is a generally consistent decline to be seen in ethnic identification over the generations, with some variations between that of the foreign-born who came to the United States before and after World War II. In the responses to the remaining items ethnicity also tends to decline, except among the second generation

FIGURE 5.1

Group Cohesiveness Scale

Please respond to all of the questions below by putting a number, from 1 to 6, in the box next to each item. The numbers range from 1 (strongly agree) to 6 (strongly disagree) as indicated in the following scale.

1	2	3	4	5	6
Strongly Agree	Agree	Mildly Agree	Mildly Disagree	Disagree	Strongly Disagree

1. The public schools should teach more about the contributions of Polish people to America. — C
2. I feel more comfortable in a Polish church. — RA
3. We don't need stronger organizations to express the views of Polish-Americans. — N
4. A Polish neighborhood is a friendlier place to live. — N
5. Organizations which carry on the Polish culture are important. — C
6. Polish religious education is not important for our children. — RC
7. Polish music makes me want to dance. — C
8. Our people should get their families to the Polish church on Sundays. — RC
9. A feeling for the Polish people is "in the blood." — N
10. Southern California does not need a Polish newspaper. — C
11. You should belong to the Polish church even if it is far from your home. — RA
12. It is not all right to change your name. — N
13. I feel more comfortable with Polish people. — N
14. We don't need centers where our young people can learn about the Polish culture. — C
15. The Polish religious tradition helps to strengthen my family life. — RA

1	2	3	4	5	6
Strongly Agree	Agree	Mildly Agree	Mildly Disagree	Disagree	Strongly Disagree

C = Cultural; N = National; RA = Religious associational; RC = Religious communal.

1	2	3	4	5	6
Strongly Agree	Agree	Mildly Agree	Mildly Disagree	Disagree	Strongly Disagree

16.	We don't need to know the history of the Polish people.	C
17.	I would rather attend a Polish Mass at Christmas.	RA
18.	Polish jokes bother me.	N
19.	It is important for me to contribute my time, talent, and finances to the Polish church.	RC
20.	If you're in trouble, you cannot count on Polish people to help you.	N
21.	We should be willing to give money to preserve the Polish tradition.	C
22.	It is better to marry someone of your own nationality.	N
23.	I should not encourage others to belong to the Polish church.	RC
24.	Our children should learn Polish dances and music.	C
25.	I prefer a church where services are in the Polish language.	RA
26.	It is too bad that the Polish tradition is not being carried on by many of our young people.	C
27.	I would vote for a Polish political candidate rather than any other nationality regardless of political party.	N
28.	Our children should learn to speak Polish.	C
29.	I don't have an obligation to help new people in the Polish parish get settled.	RC
30.	You can be for your own people first and still be a good American.	N

1	2	3	4	5	6
Strongly Agree	Agree	Mildly Agree	Mildly Disagree	Disagree	Strongly Disagree

C = Cultural; N = National; RA = Religious associational; RC = Religious communal.

TABLE 5.19

Scale Items Showing Mean Levels of
Ethnic Identification by Social Class Groups

Item Number and Classification	Upper Class	Middle Class	Working Class
1 (C)	2.24	2.43	2.19
2 (RA)	3.41	3.70	2.72
3 (N)	3.82	3.87	4.28
4 (N)	3.88	3.45	2.83
5 (C)	1.94	2.11	1.85
6 (RC)	3.41	4.28	4.09
7 (C)	2.53	2.34	1.94
8 (RC)	3.41	3.43	2.89
9 (N)	3.24	2.98	2.11
10 (C)	4.06	4.04	4.47
11 (RA)	3.94	3.79	3.13
12 (N)	3.59	3.55	2.89
13 (N)	3.12	3.87	2.83
14 (C)	4.82	4.43	4.72
15 (RA)	3.06	3.19	2.49
16 (C)	5.00	5.00	5.04
17 (RA)	2.65	3.04	2.11
18 (N)	3.24	3.83	2.91
19 (RC)	3.94	3.81	3.11
20 (N)	4.12	4.77	4.34
21 (C)	2.41	2.81	2.32
22 (N)	2.47	3.47	2.51
23 (RC)	3.47	3.81	3.94
24 (C)	2.24	2.26	1.89
25 (RA)	3.71	3.81	3.09
26 (C)	2.65	2.68	2.02
27 (N)	4.35	5.04	4.09
28 (C)	2.24	2.51	1.96
29 (RC)	3.65	3.81	3.66
30 (N)	3.12	3.06	2.19

C = Cultural; N = National; RA = Religious associational; RC = Religious communal.
Source: Compiled by the author.

TABLE 5.20

Scale Items Showing Mean Levels of Ethnic Identification by Generational Groups

Item Number and Classification	FB PRE 2	FB POS 2	2 GEN AB	3 GEN AB	4 GEN AB	ALL FOR	ALL AME
1 (C)	1.80	2.37	1.98	2.78	3.00	2.12	2.23
2 (RA)	2.40	2.32	3.02	4.22	4.67	2.35	3.30
3 (N)	4.60	4.74	4.14	3.35	3.17	4.68	3.56
4 (N)	3.20	2.42	3.31	3.65	3.67	2.76	3.23
5 (C)	1.87	1.74	1.64	2.30	3.00	1.79	1.77
6 (RC)	4.33	4.68	4.14	3.78	3.00	4.53	3.73
7 (C)	1.60	2.79	1.74	2.65	2.75	2.26	1.92
8 (RC)	2.53	2.79	3.12	3.65	4.08	2.68	3.18
9 (N)	2.27	2.21	2.33	3.13	4.00	4.24	2.51
10 (C)	4.33	4.95	4.45	3.74	3.08	4.68	3.88
11 (RA)	2.67	3.32	3.33	4.04	4.67	3.03	3.39
12 (N)	3.33	2.05	3.40	3.74	3.83	2.62	3.38
13 (N)	3.00	2.16	3.36	4.04	4.00	2.53	3.43
14 (C)	4.67	5.21	4.88	4.13	3.58	4.97	4.22
15 (RA)	2.13	2.42	2.55	3.48	4.50	2.29	2.95
16 (C)	4.87	5.47	5.21	4.83	4.17	5.21	4.79
17 (RA)	2.00	1.53	2.24	3.52	4.42	1.74	2.60
18 (N)	3.20	2.26	3.17	4.13	4.42	2.68	3.32
19 (RC)	3.20	3.32	2.95	4.22	5.00	3.26	3.32
20 (N)	3.80	4.79	4.40	4.87	4.42	4.35	4.25
21 (C)	2.53	2.00	2.05	3.26	3.75	2.24	2.36
22 (N)	2.53	1.74	2.45	4.17	4.42	2.09	2.94
23 (RC)	3.93	4.11	4.12	3.13	3.42	4.03	3.51
24 (C)	1.80	1.95	1.76	2.61	2.92	1.88	1.95
25 (RA)	2.67	2.32	3.26	4.61	5.00	2.47	3.53
26 (C)	2.00	2.05	1.95	2.91	4.00	2.03	2.23
27 (N)	4.27	3.79	4.40	5.17	5.25	4.00	4.51
28 (C)	2.27	1.68	1.74	2.91	3.50	1.94	2.06
29 (RC)	3.80	4.11	3.83	3.52	3.00	3.97	3.42
30 (N)	2.13	1.89	2.55	3.30	4.08	2.00	2.70

C = Cultural; N = National; RA = Religious associational; RC = Religious communal.
Source: Compiled by the author.

American-born, who were frequently as ethnic as the foreign-born on a variety of subjects.

When the data are assessed in terms of the cultural, national, and religio-ethnic subconstructs, very strong interest is displayed in cultural (5, 7, 21, 24, 26, 28) and religious communal areas (19, 23, 29). The generally positive ethnic response of the second generation suggests that Hansen's Law may not be valid or that it has been affected by a recent resurgence of ethnic interest.

When the data are analyzed according to foreign and American-born categories the foreign group is more ethnic in 28 of the 30 items. It is only with respect to Polish culture (5) and a feeling for Polish music (7) that the American-born showed slightly more positive feelings.

Of special interest is the relatively uniform rejection by all groups of the notion that you cannot count on Polish people for help if you're in trouble (20). Since this is a challenge to the feelings of Poles for one another, it may be a meaningful barometer of ethnic compassion at a profound level of emotional response.

The decrease in ethnic interest is also denoted by the number of individual items in which the generations showed disagreement toward the measures of ethnicity. There was no disagreement on any item among the foreign-born or the second generation, other than the unwillingness to vote for a political candidate solely because he is Polish (27), a response common to all the groups.

In the third generation, however, there were 13 items of disagreement, with the number rising to 21 in the fourth. The third generation responded negatively to 7 religious items (2, 8, 11, 17, 19, 23, 25) and 6 national items (3, 4, 12, 13, 18, 22), but was on the agreement side for all of the cultural statements. The fourth generation disagreed with all of the religious, 8 of the national (3, 4, 9, 12, 13, 18, 22, 30), and 3 of the cultural items (10, 21, 26).

These responses generally indicated only mild disagreement with the ethnic scale items. This suggests the likelihood of a reduced but ongoing degree of ethnic concern in the third and fourth generations.

SUMMARY

This chapter has presented a summary of the data analyses that have facilitated examination of the tenability of their respective null hypotheses. In the analysis of the answers to the research questions, a number of different independent variables pertaining to generations and social classes were found to be significant. Analysis of the scale items was also offered in terms of generational and social class differences.

Interpretations of these statistical results are presented in Chapter 6.

6

INTERPRETATIONS, CONCLUSIONS, AND RECOMMENDATIONS

This chapter interprets the data analyses and relates them to the research question and area of study within the framework of the theory structure established in Chapters 1 and 2. The results are examined in relation to the generational and social-class groupings, and conclusions are drawn from these interpretations, with recommendations presented pertaining to social policy.

INTERPRETATION OF GENERATIONAL DIFFERENCES

The varied perceptions of social scientists regarding changes in ethnicity over generations provided a broad theoretical context within which the research hypotheses of the current study were examined. Changing concepts of assimilation and acculturation were identified, ranging from the biological amalgamation of the "melting pot" theory to the continuity of life in both the ethnic subgroup and the larger society known as "cultural pluralism." This latter view was supported by a recognition of the critical structural factors that are necessary for the maintenance of a viable communal existence, especially in areas such as Los Angeles where kinships have not been developed within the physical proximity of an enclave.

Assimilation and acculturation were examined further through an assessment of differing views of the predicted decline or resurgence of ethnicity. The theory of Gans that there is a "straight line" reduction of ethnic consciousness was seen as a basis for the research hypothesis that ethnicity tends to decline generationally.

It was also acknowledged that a number of social and psychological factors influence changes in group cohesiveness, including acceptance of the group by those of the majority culture, and the changing patterns of an

67

increasingly mobile society. The complexity of the ethnic dimension was emphasized by those who believed that an early identity crisis and the rejection of one's past are often followed by a return later in life.

The development of a group cohesiveness scale based on the interrelatedness of religious, national, and cultural elements has been an essential factor in this study. Since one of the critical variables was believed to be the length of residence in this country, the research instrument was designed to measure changes in ethnicity in successive generations.

An examination of the results of the statistical analyses based on this scale shows that there are recognizable empirical differences between many of the generational groupings and that some of them are statistically significant. It is clear for the most part that mean levels of ethnicity as measured by the scale tend to decline over generations.

The decline is not perfectly linear, however, particularly between the third and fourth generations, where ethnic cohesiveness tends to level off to such a degree that the change is no longer statistically significant, although it should be noted that a larger fourth generation sample might have resulted in a significant difference from the third generation.

A further subtlety is the differential between the foreign-born and the second generation American-born, when the foreign-born are separated according to those who came to America before and after World War II. When the foreign-born are viewed as a single population or as a post-World War II immigrant subgroup, they are significantly different from the second generation. However, while the pre World War II immigrants are also more ethnic than the second generation, the difference is not statistically significant.

Despite the anticipated differences between the pre- and post-World War II foreign-born categories, these groups appear to be largely the same population in terms of ethnic identity. It is only in the area of national identity that a meaningful difference is apparent, which may be a consequence of distinctions between the strong national consciousness of recent immigrants, many of whom are political refugees, and those who have been acculturated by a longer American experience.

Additional distinctions arise in an examination of the generations in terms of the religious, national, and cultural variables. Religious identification is extremely high, with most of the respondents placing themselves in the Roman Catholic group. However, differences emerge when membership in a church is distinguished from merely nominal identification with it. These differences are further complicated by an assessment of membership in the Polish and non-Polish churches; the data suggest that as membership in the Polish churches decreases in each generation, membership in the non-Polish churches increases, except in the fourth generation where religious involvement is generally low. An interesting distinction, however, is made between religio-ethnic attitudes as measured by the ethnic scale, which remain fairly high in the second generation, and religio-ethnic behavior, which changes substantially, as evidenced by greatly reduced membership in the Polish churches.

Cultural ethnicity remains consistently strong in both foreign-born groups and the second generation, with virtually no change in cultural scale scores. Between the second and third generations, however, a significant difference becomes apparent. The fourth generation is less ethnic culturally than the third, but the difference is not statistically significant. National ethnicity scores are reduced successively across the generations, with all differences significant except between the third and fourth generations.

A summary of the statistical interpretations of these variables suggests that there are a number of differences between the generational categories in terms of the salience of ethnicity. Hence, in answering the research question from a statistical point of view it may be said that there appears to be a relationship between the salience of ethnicity and the generational groups.

This is manifested in the statistically significant differences observed between the foreign-born, second, and third generations in the total ethnicity construct. It is also shown in the patterns of change evidenced generationally in the religious, cultural, and national subconstructs.

INTERPRETATION OF SOCIAL CLASS DIFFERENCES

The relatedness of ethnic and social class factors was also assessed in order to facilitate an examination of the second research hypothesis that the salience of ethnicity was inversely related to social class.

Theoretical perceptions were identified that focused on three key areas of interest. The view was advanced that ethnicity is a paramount value that influences the patterns of association of individuals of the same group, although they often confine their primary-group social participation to the "ethclass," the social class segment within their own ethnic group.

Another view was the assumption that most ethnics of the second, third, and subsequent generations are leaving their neighborhood enclaves and moving to heterogeneous suburbs where group identification is less relevant; consequently it was believed that social class groupings are becoming cross-ethnic, particularly in the sprawling environment of Los Angeles. This geographical dispersion has been particularly evident among the Polish-Americans in Los Angeles, who had not created a primary ethnic neighborhood even in the period of early settlement.

The problem was highlighted by the belief that America permits and encourages upward mobility and that this may be very disruptive to the ethnic group, since an increasingly affluent society may foster greater social and geographical mobility, thereby contributing to the decline of ethnic cohesion.

A middle position that offered an alternative to separatism or assimilation was identified. This posited the emergence of a new kind of ethnic group that has found a way to maintain its identity in the diverse environment of suburbia through the utilization of reference group associations and modern techniques of communication.

The creation of a typology of socioeconomic status was a necessary element in the stratification and placement of individuals in the sample. This facilitated the measurement of changes in ethnic cohesiveness according to social class, an essential precondition for examination of the research hypothesis.

An assessment of the results of the empirical analyses indicates that there are identifiable differences between a number of the social class groupings and that some of them are statistically significant. The working class is significantly more ethnic than either the middle or the upper classes. It is also apparent that the middle and upper classes appear to approximate one another closely in terms of ethnic identity.

If it is assumed that the middle and upper classes are essentially the same population, or if they are treated separately in relation to the working class, the research hypothesis suggesting that ethnicity varies inversely with social class is supported. Consequently, the rising socioeconomic status typical of American life may portend a reduction in the holding power of the working class ethnic group. This may be particularly relevant for Polish-Americans in Los Angeles, whose suburban life style and growing affluence identify them with the traits of upward social mobility in America.

Consequently, the data analyses of both the generational and the social class variables tend to support the research hypotheses in the context of the theory structure that has been presented. As a result, additional insights are provided for dealing with the problem of ethnic continuity and its future in a pluralistic American society.

CONCLUSIONS

A number of conclusions may be drawn from this study of ethnic group cohesiveness. These pertain to the length of time the Polish-American group has been in the United States as reflected in generational differences, the relatedness of social class and mobility, and the impact of psycho-social factors on identity.

It seems likely that the processes of assimilation and acculturation continue to be operative, and that Polish-Americans in the Los Angeles Metropolitan Area tend to be less ethnic over generations. This conclusion may be extended with caution to the Polish-American population in Southern California and probably to the entire state. However, generalizations about the national scene pertaining to Polish and non-Polish ethnic groups should be considered somewhat speculative.

Although the decline in ethnicity gives support to the theory of Gans that there is a more or less "straight line" decrease over generations, some distinctions must be made concerning the future of group life in America.

It is important to note that ethnicity is measurable into the fourth generation, suggesting that it continues to have meaning in the lives of large numbers of people. This is supported by the fact that differences between the third and fourth generations are not significant and may signify either a leveling off of the loss of identification or a resurgence of ethnic interest.

A further consideration is the relative similarity between the foreign-born who came here before World War II and the second generation American-born. Comparisons between these groups are important because an examination of parent-child relationships is possible uncontaminated by the inclusion of the later immigrants.

Although mean levels of ethnic identification are stronger for the earlier foreign-born group, the differences between them and the second generation are not significant. This may lead to the conclusion that the critical decline in ethnicity of the second generation posited by Hansen did not take place or that there has been a resurgence of ethnicity as hypothesized by Glazer and others.

It seems apparent that the children, grandchildren, and great-grand-children of Polish immigrants take a substantial interest in the culture and traditions of their forefathers. Nonetheless an erosion of ethnicity has taken place as a consequence of the pressures of Anglo-conformity and because of new patterns of living. Hence, a resurgence of ethnic interest among them may result in an expression of a marginal ethnicity altered to meet the requirements of the larger culture.

The perceived shift in ethnic identification may be seen most clearly in the religious area, where the data indicate a decline in religio-ethnic behavior, as evidenced by a drop in Polish church membership over generations. At the same time religio-ethnic attitudes also tend to decline, but less appreciably, with a significant difference shown only between the second and third generations.

This dichotomy between attitudes and behavior suggests the possibility that suburban living has made attendance at the Polish church less convenient, perhaps because of the great distances many have to travel in the Los Angeles area. Consequently many individuals may limit their participation in Polish church services to major holidays and celebrations without maintaining actual membership in the church. This notion is supported by the data, which indicate a declining but continuing pattern of attendance at the Polish church.

On the other hand, the data show a regular increase in non-Polish church membership and attendance until the fourth generation, where it drops markedly. While this apparent shift to the non-ethnic church could indicate support for the Herberg thesis, some important differences must be considered.

Although membership in the Polish churches drops sharply in the second generation, almost half of the respondents have continued their membership, and many express strong religio-ethnic attitudes. Moreover, Polish church attendance is higher in the second generation than among the pre-World War II foreign-born, the presumed parent generation.

In addition, there is a sharp drop in religious interest in the fourth generation in terms of membership in both the Polish and non-Polish churches, as well as in attendance at services. Herberg's hypothesis that the second generation rejects the ethnic church is not confirmed by this; nor is his belief that there is a growing religious interest beyond the third generation.

The data of the current study are more consistent with the Lenski findings, which point to a pattern of increasing religious involvement into the third generation. However, neither Lenski nor Herberg give adequate consideration to the ethnic factor, and both tend to assume a relatively homogeneous Catholic population limited only by race.

The change in religio-ethnic behavior should be seen in the context of a decreasing but still measurable interest in the national church. While shifting social and demographic patterns are influencing the traditional closeness of church and community, the ethnic church may serve as the symbolic reference point for a population that continues to live in two worlds.

This view is supported by the fact that many Polish-Americans maintain dual memberships in the Polish and non-Polish churches. It is also indicated by the expression of an ongoing interest in Polish religious symbols and practices as evidenced by the responses of all the generations in the religious subscale.

It is apparent that generational differences alone do not sufficiently explain the changes in cohesiveness of ethnic groups. Other critical elements in the acculturation process include higher social status and increased social mobility, factors that often go together.

The data on Polish-Americans in the Los Angeles Metropolitan Area tend to support the hypothesis that social class is inversely related to the salience of ethnicity. Hence there is the likelihood that the rise in societal affluence is contributing to a decline of ethnic continuity in America.

From this conclusion, inferences may be drawn with caution about the population of Polonia in Southern California and perhaps about the entire state, however, generalizations about the national population of Polish and non-Polish ethnic groups should be viewed as conjectural.

Although gains in socioeconomic status portend a reduction in ethnic identification, certain factors may modify this process. These include the changing patterns of those who migrated to Los Angeles and the emergence of new means of communication within the group, and may be explained in the following way.

Polish-Americans came to the Los Angeles area from other parts of the country and from Poland in large numbers because of economic opportunities and the pleasant climate. The move may have been accompanied by some loss of ethnic contact and involvement, especially in a large geographical setting where people tended to live near their work rather than near their kin.

While there were and are some small enclaves in different parts of the metropolitan area, the tendency has been to disperse. This perception is supported by the data presented in Chapter 2 and by Census tract data in the Appendix, which show Polish-Americans living in widely scattered places. Among these are some persons for whom the migration to California may have represented an opportunity to assimilate into the larger culture in order to lose an identity that no longer met their needs.

The pattern of mobility has probably been accompanied by a shift from the extended family of the ethnic enclave, as defined by neighborhood boundaries and familial obligations, to the geographical fluidity of the nuclear family, together with its changing system of values. The patriarchal tradition of the peasant family has disintegrated as wives joined the work force, daughters sought equality of the sexes, and marriage became a matter of individual choice.

Moreover, as increasing numbers of Polish-Americans have accepted the ideals and practices of the middle and upper-middle classes there was a growth of individualism, whereby one's interests were less identified with the fortunes of the family. This different outlook, which was influenced by social mobility, undoubtedly contributed to the gap between the generations, particularly as it was manifested in the decline of group cohesiveness.

The mobile, culturally diverse, tradition-free environment of Los Angeles was a forerunner of the suburban milieu that was to emerge elsewhere a generation or more later. To maintain ethnic communication, new modes of in-group association were needed in order to preserve friendships and extended family ties over a wide area. Friends and families were now linked by the automobile and the telephone, the indispensable links of contemporary urban life as well as by the religious, cultural, charitable, and social institutions of the Los Angeles Polonia.

Etzioni and Parenti called attention to the emergence of a meaningful ethnic communal life in suburbia, a culture that was transplanted from the neighborhood enclave. In an area where neighbors might be from any group, new structural arrangements were developed based on social ties and psychological needs rather than on the physical proximity of the enclave.

Supporting their confidence in the future of ethnicity in suburbia was the belief that middle-class life styles did not destroy the vitality of ethnic associations. The growing affluence of ethnic groups was seen as an important element in the building of subgroup structures that enabled them to maintain the preferred companionship of the primary group.

Thus what is happening to Polish-Americans in Los Angeles may be comparable to developments elsewhere in suburbia. At the same time the patterns pioneered by the Los Angeles Polonia have been reinforced as the group has become more prosperous and has tended to adopt the values of the middle class. This was accelerated by the higher educational levels of Polish-Americans in the West mentioned in Chapter 2.

The shift to a suburban life style can be seen as a process of social change and adjustment in which ethnicity has diminished considerably but continues to be a factor in the lives of many people. The bond of identity is expressed through formal and informal structural associations and maintained by a common history and tradition. It may also be supported by the currently fashionable voicing of ethnic identification and pride, as well as by the emergence of a new militancy resulting from the abrasiveness of intergroup contacts and perceptions.

On the other hand it should be remembered that attitudes within Polonia may also be influenced by feelings of shame or self-consciousness about Polish identity, the result of living in a society that has given relatively little recognition or respect to those of Polish ancestry, and in which Polish people have been stereotyped as stupid, clumsy, vulgar, and racist.

This comparatively hostile climate, combined with a failure to appreciate their own heritage, has made many Polish-Americans feel inferior and seek to disappear into the larger culture. This has often been manifested in the widespread practice of name changing, which is viewed with mixed feelings by the community: while some object to any modification of the family name, others see a change as a necessary response to prejudice, as a means of gaining economic advantage, as a way of overcoming pronunciation or spelling difficulty, or as a way of hiding their national origin.

This may be viewed in the context of cognitive dissonance, an uncomfortable psychological condition that motivates a person to try to reduce the dissonance and achieve consonance. Since Polish-Americans are often perceived as a low status group, this may produce feelings of dissonance among some, and result in efforts to reduce or eliminate it. Hence the person may conceal his background or avoid situations that are likely to embarrass him. The latter situation, however, may also tend to strengthen ethnic identification by causing an individual to limit his associations to others like himself.

An essential function of group identity is to assure self-acceptance and self-esteem. When the status of a group is such that it contributes to the self-rejection of an individual, it becomes a serious problem, and often a matter of personal crisis, for many of its members, since the success or failure of an individual's identity structure may be directly related to the status of his group in society. In the current study the relevance of this situation to group continuity may have been evidenced by the number of college students approached for interviews who seemed to be unwilling to acknowledge that they had Polish backgrounds.

One of the chief concerns in Polonia is with the good name of the community; members want to be accepted and admired by the American people and to have their achievements and patriotism recognized. There is often bitter resentment of ridicule of the group and particularly of Polish jokes. This sensitivity was revealed early in the planning of this study, when fears were expressed by Polish leaders that the research project might be anti-Polish and injure the reputation of Polonia.

A summary of the conclusions emanating from this study suggests that the investigation has accomplished its purpose; that a useful contribution has been made to the solution of the problem under consideration; and that the theoretical literature on the relative depth and longevity of ethnic identity has been expanded. It is apparent that generational and social class factors are related to the future of ethnic groups, and that there is a decline in ethnicity over time, especially in an upwardly mobile society. It is also evident that the loss of ethnic holding power is substantially influenced by the impact of status considerations in a society that values some groups more than others.

An ameliorating factor, however, is the heightened interest in group life in America, which has given support to those who continue to value their ethnic traditions and others who have developed a new appreciation of them. A consequence of this phenomenon may be the emergence of new forms of ethnic identification and communication, which enable the growing numbers of ethnics residing in suburban settings to maintain group continuity.

RECOMMENDATIONS

There is widespread interest in the ethnic dimension, and it seems evident that additional research is needed, especially as it pertains to social policy considerations. This will be particularly helpful as public and private agencies concerned with strengthening group life and reducing intergroup tensions consider their goals and priorities for the future.

It will be important, therefore, to evaluate further the decline or resurgence of ethnicity in terms of the effects of social, psychological, economic, and political factors. These include a number of relevant questions that may provide a basis for future research efforts.

1. Do people give up their ethnic identity because it no longer has meaning for them or because the general culture ascribes a lower status to their group?
2. Is the alienation resulting from a mass, technological, urban society strengthening or diluting ethnic commitment?
3. What are the differential rates of assimilation in the suburban and enclave environments?
4. Is cultural assimilation proceeding more rapidly than structural assimilation?
5. What is the relationship between ethnicity and such societal issues as racial integration, voting patterns, social welfare, the counter-culture, and the environment?
6. Are separatism and community control in conflict with the interests of the larger society?
7. Since ethnics may be lacking in political power, are they vulnerable to exotic social and political movements?
8. How does the existence of intergroup hostility affect the potential for cross-ethnic movements?
9. What is the relationship between group cohesiveness and the institutional life of the ethnic community?
10. To what extent do ethnics with high group cohesiveness associate with others outside the group?
11. Is there a differential rate of upward social mobility among the various ethnic groups in our society?
12. What is the relationship between the geographical mobility of ethnics and their socioeconomic status?

The group cohesiveness scale developed in the current study should be a useful instrument in the furtherance of research efforts among ethnic groups, especially those who have emigrated from European countries where there is a distinct national history, culture, and religion. With relatively minor adjustments to the instrument, according to the unique characteristics of the particular group, it seems likely that distinct and meaningful empirical differences can be observed that will aid in examining such variables as intermarriage, church attendance, political behavior, and some of the other factors referred to above.

It would be helpful, however, to test the scale with larger samples as well as with those groups living in Eastern enclaves, who may be different from the dispersed ethnics of Los Angeles. Further, it should be noted that the ex post facto research design imposed limitations as described by Kerlinger (1964), including the lack of control over independent variables; the inability to randomize because of prior self-selection; and, as a result of these weaknesses, the risk of improper interpretation and generalization.

An additional recommendation is the development of comparative studies within Polonia itself in cities like Detroit, Michigan, where the Polish enclave is still viable. A research project concerning the presumed differences between enclave and suburban life styles, as well as the future potential of the Polish group under these differing circumstances, would be helpful. It may well be that repeated studies at regular time intervals would shed light on the changing characteristics of group life for Polish-Americans and others, and help to predict how long they will survive as distinct entities in our multicultural environment.

The social policy implications of these analyses are clear, for we live in a society with a mass culture that tends to homogenize and work against ethnic continuity. What may be needed are publicly sanctioned vehicles for ethnic distinctiveness that provide both facilities for cultural enrichment and an atmosphere that encourages diversity within the framework of American unity.

Although it has not as yet been funded, the Ethnic Heritage Act recently adopted by the Congress is an example of the kind of public input that may help to overcome the prevailing view that ethnic variations are foreign and that they should be absorbed within the larger culture. The development of ethnic cultural centers, support of foreign languages in the public schools, and overseas exchange programs are all needed, but on a much larger scale than at present. Thus, by providing recognition for ethnicity at the highest levels of national policy and programming a climate may be established that is truly hospitable to difference.

The reassertion of identity is also affected by the willingness and ability of private ethnic institutions to develop collective action in their approach to the problems of life. Although there are numerous organizations in Polonia, for the most part they are geared to such matters as securing better treatment in the media and developing political support for freedom in Poland. While these are important considerations, they do not take the place of assistance to the aged, youth counseling, and helping families with special needs.

Despite these pressing requirements, substantial sums of money are spent on public celebrations and on national symbols of ethnic pride such as the restoration of castles in Poland. Moreover, relatively large resources are apparently left untapped in the insurance funds of fraternal groups, which could be used for housing, medical care, and other programs.

This situation may be explained in part by the absence of a national tradition of group responsibility, which makes it difficult for Polish-Americans to join together cooperatively. It may also reflect reluctance to admit the existence of problems that could lead to a loss of prestige.

Despite the fragmentation of Polish institutional life and the individualism of Polish-Americans, there appears to be an increase in the effectiveness of collaborative action in such groups as the Polish American Congress, which is seeking to influence public policy in behalf of the interests of Polonia. However, unifying goals and programs are also needed to make institutions within Polonia more effective.

This is particularly evident in Los Angeles, which has some forty diverse Polish-American organizations, but where the fact that no directory of groups has been published since 1950 suggests the existence of a community organization gap. The problem is also manifested in the critical lack of support for Polish cultural creativity and for such needs as social and psychological research.

A further dimension is the limited support of Polish education and scholarship, which suffer not only from a lack of funding but from the inadequate involvement of Polish-American students in the pursuance of careers related to the intellectual and social requirements of Polonia. This is not to suggest, however, that only an individual of a particular group can understand his own people; often an outsider has a perspective that is unimpaired by in-group loyalties.

While it is difficult to predict how much longer ethnic groups will survive in America, the fact is that ethnic interest is a reality that will be with us for some time to come. This is evident in the Polonia of Los Angeles, where a suburban prototype of the ethnic may have developed, an upwardly mobile individual with a new and meaningful life style.

What may be needed for the future, however, is an ethnic ideology that accepts the existence of group interests and needs but recognizes that in America only the individual has rights. With this approach it may be possible to validate the legitimacy of group attachments while avoiding the dangers of ethnocentrism. This may appeal to the self-perception of the changing Polish-American and offer a means for assuring group survival.

REFERENCES

Books

Abramson, Harold J. *Ethnic Pluralism in the Central City*. Storrs, Conn.: Institute for Urban Research of the University of Connecticut, 1970.

Baltzell, E. Digby. *The Protestant Establishment: Aristocracy and Caste in America*. New York: Vintage Books, 1964.

Blalock, Hubert M. *Social Statistics*. New York: McGraw-Hill Book Co., 1960.

Bogue, Donald J. *The Population of the United States*. New York: The Free Press of Glencoe, 1959.

Carmichael, Stokely, and Charles V. Hamilton. *Black Power: The Politics of Liberation in America*. New York: Random House, 1967.

Cole, Stewart G., and Mildred Wiese Cole. *Minorities and the American Promise*. New York: Harper and Bros., 1954.

Edwards, Allen L. *Techniques of Attitude Scale Construction*. New York: Appleton-Century-Crofts, 1957.

Festinger, Leon. *A Theory of Cognitive Dissonance*. Stanford, Calif.: Stanford University Press, 1962.

Fishman, Joshua A. *Language Loyalty in the United States*. The Hague: Mouton and Co., 1966.

Friedman, Murray. *Overcoming Middle Class Rage*. Philadelphia: The Westminster Press, 1971.

Gans, Herbert J. *The Urban Villagers*. New York: The Free Press, 1962.

Glazer, Nathan. "Ethnic Groups in America: From National Culture to Ideology." *Freedom and Control in Modern Society*. Edited by Berger, Abel, and Page. New York: D. Van Nostrand Company, Inc., 1954.

————, and Daniel Patrick Moynihan. *Beyond the Melting Pot*. Cambridge, Mass.: M.I.T. Press, 1970.

Gordon, Milton M. *Assimilation in American Life*. New York: Oxford University Press, 1964.

Graham, Hugh Davis, and Ted Robert Gurr. *The History of Violence in America*. New York: Bantam Books, 1969.

Greeley, Andrew M., and Peter H. Rossi. *The Education of Catholic Americans*. Garden City, N.Y.: Anchor Books, 1968.

Haiman, Miecislaus. *Polish Past in America—1608-1865*. Chicago: The Polish Roman Catholic Union Archives and Museum, 1939.

Hall, Calvin S., and Gardner Lindzey. *Theories of Personality*. New York: John Wiley and Sons, 1970.

Handlin, Oscar. *The Uprooted*. New York: Grossett and Dunlap, 1951.

Herberg, Will. *Protestant-Catholic-Jew*. Garden City, N.Y.: Anchor Books, 1960.

Hollingshead, August B., and Frederick C. Redlich. *Social Class and Mental Illness: A Community Study*. New York: John Wiley and Sons, 1958.

Hutchinson, Edward P. *Immigrants and Their Children*. New York: John Wiley and Sons, 1956.

Jones, Maldwyn Allen. *American Immigration*. Chicago: University of Chicago Press, 1960.

Kallen, Horace M. *Culture and Democracy in the United States*. New York: Boni and Liveright, 1924.

Kerlinger, Fred N. *Foundations of Behavioral Research*. New York: Holt, Rinehart and Winston, 1964.

Kruszka, Waclaw. *Historja Polakow w Ameryce*. Milwaukee: Kuryer Publishing Company, 1905.

Lenski, Gerhard. *The Religious Factor*. Garden City, N.Y.: Anchor Books, 1963.

Lieberson, Stanley. *Ethnic Patterns in American Cities*. New York: The Free Press of Glencoe, 1963.

Lopata, Helena Znaniecki. "The Function of Voluntary Associations in an Ethnic Community: 'Polonia'." *Contributions to Urban Sociology*. Edited by Ernest W. Burgess and Donald J. Bogue. Chicago: University of Chicago Press, 1964.

Maisel, Albert Q. *They All Chose America*. New York: Thomas Nelson and Sons, 1955.

Marden, Charles F., and Gladys Meyer. *Minorities in American Society*. New York: The Van Nostrand Reinhold Co., 1968.

Merton, Robert K. *Social Theory and Social Structure*. New York: The Free Press, 1957.

Murphy, G., and R. Likert. *Public Opinion and the Individual*. New York: Harper and Bros., 1937.

Olszyk, Edmund G. *The Polish Press in America*. Milwaukee: Marquette University Press, 1940.

Rosten, Leo. *Religions in America*. New York: Simon and Schuster, 1963.

Roucek, Joseph S., and Francis J. Brown. *Our Racial and National Minorities.* New York: Prentice Hall, 1937.

Steiner, Stan. *The New Indians.* New York: Dell Publishing Co., 1968.

Super, Paul. *The Polish Tradition.* London: Maxlove Publishing Company, Ltd., 1939.

Thomas, William I., and Florian Znaniecki. *The Polish Peasant in Europe and America*, 5 Vols. Boston: The Gorham Press, 1918-20.

Warner, W. Lloyd. *American Life.* Chicago: University Chicago Press, 1953.

————, and Leo Srole. *The Social Systems of American Ethnic Groups.* New Haven: Yale University Press, 1945.

White, Leslie A. *The Evolution of Culture.* New York: McGraw-Hill Book Co., 1959.

Wirth, Louis. *On Cities and Social Life.* Edited by Albert J. Reiss, Jr. Chicago: University of Chicago Press, 1964.

Wood, Arthur Evans. *Hamtramck—A Sociological Study of a Polish American Community.* New Haven: College and University Press, 1955.

Wytrwal, Joseph A. *America's Polish Heritage.* Detroit: Endurance Press, 1961.

————. *Poles in American History and Tradition.* Detroit: Endurance Press, 1969.

Zangwill, Israel. *The Melting Pot.* New York: The Macmillan Co., 1909.

Periodicals

Abramson, Harold J., and C. Edward Noll. "Religion, Ethnicity and Social Change." *The Review of Religious Research* (Fall 1966).

Bender, Eugene I., and George Kagiwada. "Hansen's Law of Third Generation Return and the Study of American Religious Ethnic Groups." *Phylon* 29, no. 4 (Winter 1968).

Borhek, J. T. "Ethnic-Group Cohesion." *The American Journal of Sociology* 76, no. 1 (July 1970).

Carpenter, Niles, and Daniel Katz. "The Cultural Adjustment of the Polish Group in the City of Buffalo: An Experiment in the Technique of Social Investigation." *Social Forces* 6, nos. 1-4 (September 1927).

Elzearia, M. "Notes on Polish American Music." *Polish American Studies* 11, nos. 1-2 (January-June 1954).

Etzioni, Amitai. "The Ghetto—A Re-evaluation." *Social Forces* 37, no. 3 (March 1959).

Gans, Herbert. "American Jewry: Present and Future." *Commentary* 21, no. 5 (May 1956).

————. "The Future of American Jewry: Part II." *Commentary* 21, no. 6 (June 1956).

Glazer, Nathan. "America's Ethnic Pattern—Melting Pot or Nation of Nations?" *Commentary* 15, no. 4 (April 1953).

Goering, John M. "The Emergence of Ethnic Interests: A Case of Serendipity." *Social Forces* 49, no. 3 (March 1971).

Green, Arnold W. "A Re-examination of the Marginal Man Concept." *Social Forces* 26, nos. 1-4 (December 1947).

Greene, Victor R. "For God and Country: The Origins of Slavic-Catholic Self-Consciousness in America." *Church History* 35, no. 4 (December 1966).

Greer, Scott. "Catholic Voters and the Democratic Party." *Public Opinion Quarterly* (Winter 1961).

Hansen, Marcus L. "The Third Generation in America." *Commentary* 14, no. 5 (November 1952).

Hutchinson, Edward P. "The New Immigration: An Introductory Comment." *Annals of the American Academy of Political and Social Science* 367 (September 1966).

Isaacs, Harold R. "Group Identity and Political Change." *Survey* 69 (London: October 1968).

Karcz, Valerin. "The Polish American Congress 1944-1959." *Polish American Studies* 16, nos. 3-4 (July-December 1959).

Kennedy, Ruby Jo. "Single or Triple Melting Pot? Intermarriage Trends in New Haven, 1870-1940." *The American Journal of Sociology* 49, no. 4 (January 1944).

Kowalczyk, Edmund L. "James F. Reed-Rydnowski, California Pioneer." *Polish American Studies* 5, nos. 3-4 (July-December 1948).

Krickus, Richard J. "The White Ethnics: Who Are They and Where Are They Going?" *City* (May-June 1971).

Lewanski, Richard C. "California Localities Connected with Poland and Poles." *Polish American Studies* 14, nos. 1-2 (January-June 1957).

Lieberson, Stanley. "Suburbs and Ethnic Residential Patterns." *The American Journal of Sociology* 67, no. 6 (May 1962).

Madaj, M. J. "The Polish Community—A Ghetto?" *Polish American Studies* 25, no. 2 (July-December 1968).

Masuda, M., G. H. Matsumoto, and G. M. Meredith. "Ethnic Identity in Three Generations of Japanese Americans." *The Journal of Social Psychology* 81, second half (August 1970).

Monzell, Thomas I. "The Catholic Church and the Americanization of the Polish Immigrant." *Polish American Studies* 26, no. 1 (January-June 1969).

Mostwin, Danuta. "Post-World War II Polish Immigrants in the United States." *Polish American Studies* 16, no. 2 (Autumn 1969).

Parenti, Michael. "Ethnic Politics and the Persistence of Ethnic Identification." *American Political Science Review* (September 1967).

Rennig, R., L. Srole, M. Opler, and T. Langner. "Urban Life and Mental Health." *The American Journal of Psychiatry* 113, no. 9 (March 1957).

Schneider, Michael M. "Middle America: Study in Frustration." *The Center Magazine* (November-December 1970).

Seroczynski, Felix Thomas. "Poles in the United States." *The Catholic Encyclopedia*. Vol. 12. New York: McGraw-Hill Book Co., 1911.

Slesinski, Thaddeus. "Development of Cultural Activities in Polish American Communities." *Polish American Studies* 5, nos. 3-4 (July-December 1948).

Swastek, Joseph. "The Contribution of the Catholic Church in Poland to the Catholic Church in the U.S.A." *Polish American Studies* 24, no. 1 (January-June 1967).

_____. "What Is a Polish American?" *Polish American Studies* 1, (January-December 1944).

Szynczak, Miecislaus S. "Polish American Statistical Materials." *Polish American Studies* 21, no. 2 (July-December 1964).

Taeuber, Alma F., and Karl E. Taeuber. "Recent Immigration and Studies of Ethnic Assimilation." *Demography* 4, no. 2 (1967).

Thomas, John. "The New Immigration and Cultural Pluralism." *American Catholic Sociological Review* 15 (December 1954).

Thurstone, L. L. "Attitudes Can Be Measured." *The American Journal of Sociology* 33, no. 4 (January 1928).

Wagner, Stanley P. "The Polish American Vote in 1960." *Polish American Studies* 21, no. 1 (January-June 1964).

Wloszczewski, Dr. Stefan. "The Polish 'Sociological Group' in America." *American Slavic Review* (August 1945).

Zand, Helen Stankiewicz. "Polish American Profile." *Polish American Studies* 28, no. 2 (July-December 1961).

_____. "Polish Foodways in America." *Polish American Studies* 14, nos. 3-4 (July-December 1957).

_____. "Polish Institutional Folkways in the United States." *Polish American Studies* 14, nos. 1-2 (January-June 1957).

Reports

Polish American Congress, Inc., California State District. *Directory*. 1950.

————, California-Arizona Division. *Proceedings of the Fourteenth Regional Convention, Phoenix, Arizona, September 1 and 2, 1957.*

Schroeder, R. C. *Ethnic America.* Editorial Research Reports. Washington, D.C., January 20, 1971.

U.S. Bureau of the Census. *Characteristics of the Population by Ethnic Origin: November, 1969.* Current Population Reports. Washington, D.C.: Government Printing Office, 1971.

————. *City, County Data Book for Los Angeles.* Washington, D.C.: Government Printing Office, 1967.

————. *Compendium of the Tenth Census: 1880.* Washington, D.C.: Government Printing Office, 1883.

————. *Fifteenth Census of the U.S.: 1930.* Vol. 3, part 1. Washington, D.C.: Government Printing Office, 1932.

————. *Fourteenth Census of the U.S.: 1920.* Washington, D.C.: Government Printing Office, 1922.

————. *Historical Statistics of the U.S., Colonial Times to 1957.* Washington, D.C.: Government Printing Office, 1960.

————. *Sixteenth Census of the U.S.: 1940.* Vol. 2. Washington, D.C.: Government Printing Office, 1943.

————. "The Statistics of the Population of the United States." *Ninth Census of the U.S.: 1870.* Vol. 2. Washington, D.C.: Government Printing Office, 1872.

————. *Twelfth Census of the U.S.: 1900.* Population, Part 1. Washington, D.C.: Government Printing Office, 1901.

————. *U.S. Census of Population, California.* Vol. 2, part 5. Washington, D.C.: Government Printing Office, 1950.

————. *U.S. Census of Population: 1960.* Vol. 1, part 1. Washington, D.C.: Government Printing Office, 1964.

————. *U.S. Census of Population: 1960, California.* Final Report PC [1]-6D. Washington, D.C.: Government Printing Office, 1962.

————. *United States Census of Population 1960, Nativity and Parentage.* Final Report PC [2]-1A. Washington, D.C.: Government Printing Office, 1965.

————. *U.S. Census of Population: 1970.* Washington, D.C.: Government Printing Office, 1972.

Personal Interviews

Kalata, Rev. E. Interview, September, 1970.

Rydzeski, Antoinette. Interview, October, 1971.

Other

Browne, Robert S., and Bayard Rustin. *Separatism or Integration, Which Way for America?* New York: National Jewish Community Relations Advisory Council, 1968.

Danzig, David. "The Social Framework of Ethnic Conflict in America." Paper presented at Fordham University, New York, June 8, 1968.

Greeley, Andrew M. *Why Can't They Be Like Us?* New York: Institute of Human Relations Press, 1969.

Haiman, Miecislaus. *Polish Pioneers in California.* Chicago: Annals of the Polish Roman Catholic Union, 1940.

Kosberg, Milton L. "The Polish Colony of California 1876-1914." Masters thesis, University of Southern California, June 1952.

Levine, Irving M., and Judith M. Herman. *The Ethnic Factor in Blue Collar Life.* New York: The American Jewish Committee, 1971.

The Polish National Catholics. Chicago: Claretian Publications, 1965.

Polish Women's Alliance of America Constitution and By-Laws, Amended and Adopted by the XXIV Convention. Chicago: the Alliance, 1963.

Strakacz, Sylwin. "Outline of the History of the Poles in Los Angeles." *In Tribute to the Blessed Virgin of the Bright Mount.* Detroit: Globe Press, 1958.

Swastek, Joseph. *The Polish American Story.* Buffalo, N.Y.: The Felician Sisters, 1952.

Zielinski, Antony J. "Poland's Intellectual Contribution." *Poles in America, Their Contribution to a Century of Progress.* Chicago: Polish Day Association, 1933.

ADDITIONAL DESCRIPTIVE DATA

TABLE A.1

Polish Foreign Stock in the Los Angeles-Long Beach
Standard Metropolitan Statistical Area
(SMSA)

Community	Number of Polish Residents	Community	Number of Polish Residents
Long Beach	2,084	Lancaster	176
Los Angeles	44,198	Lennox	164
Alhambra	631	Lynwood	202
Altadena	285	Manhattan Beach	135
Arcadia	234	Monrovia	213
Baldwin Park	134	Montebello	328
Bellflower	126	Monterey Park	684
Bell Gardens	86	Norwalk	484
Beverly Hills	1,583	Paramount	115
Burbank	1,050	Pasadena	656
Carson	118	Pico-Rivera	268
Compton	201	Pomona	323
Culver City	720	Redondo Beach	270
Downey	539	Santa Monica	1,043
East Los Angeles	522	South Gate	450
Florence-Graham	40	South San Gabriel	162
Gardena	408	Temple City	210
Glendale	609	Torrance	740
Hawthorne	345	West Covina	492
Huntington Park	325	West Hollywood	1,700
Inglewood	665	Whittier	136
Lakewood	418	Balance	6,186

Total SMSA: 73,959*

*Some discrepancies exist for Census tracts.
Source: U.S. Census Bureau, 1960 Census tracts.

85

TABLE A.2

Distribution of Polish Foreign Stock by Numbers of Persons in Census Tracts of Selected Communities in the Los Angeles-Long Beach Standard Metropolitan Statistical Area

Community	None	Under 100	100-249	250-499	500 and Over
Los Angeles	78	506	98	18	10
Burbank	—	7	11	—	—
E. Los Angeles	2	14	1	—	—
Culver City	—	2	3	—	—
Glendale	—	22	—	—	—
Inglewood	2	10	—	—	—
Pasadena	2	28	1	—	—
South Gate	1	7	1	—	—
Torrance	—	14	1	—	—
W. Hollywood	—	—	1	3	1
Long Beach	9	60	2	—	—

Source: U.S. Census Bureau, 1960 Census tracts.

TABLE A.3

Generational Groups Categorized by Type of Residence

Generational Group	Own Home		Rent	
	Number of Respondents	Percent	Number of Respondents	Percent
FB PRE 2	11	9.9	3	2.7
FB POS 2	17	15.3	3	2.7
2 GEN AB	37	33.3	5	4.5
3 GEN AB	17	15.3	6	5.4
4 GEN AB	6	5.4	5	4.5
ALL FOR	28	25.2	6	5.4
ALL AME	60	54.1	16	14.4
Total	88	79.3	22	19.8

Note: There were no respondents in the Mobile Home category.
Source: Compiled by the author.

86

TABLE A.4

Generational Groups Categorized by Weekly Income

Generational Group	Weekly Income											
	Under $100		$100-174		$175-199		$200-249		$250-299		$300 and Over	
	Number of Respondents	Per-cent	Number of Respondents	Per-cent	Number of Respondents	Per-cent	Number of Respondents	Per-cent	Number of Respondents	Per-cent	Number of Respondents	Per-cent
FB PRE 2	2	1.8	1	0.9	—	—	1	0.9	—	—	5	4.5
FB POS 2	—	—	2	1.8	3	2.7	5	4.5	2	1.8	6	5.4
2 GEN AB	4	3.6	6	5.4	3	2.7	4	3.6	3	2.7	21	18.9
3 GEN AB	1	0.9	1	0.9	2	1.8	3	2.7	4	3.6	10	9.0
4 GEN AB	1	0.9	2	1.8	—	—	3	2.7	2	1.8	3	2.7
TOTAL	8	7.2	12	10.8	8	7.2	16	14.4	11	9.9	45	40.5

Source: Compiled by the author.

TABLE A.5

Generational Groups Categorzied by Occupation

Generational Group	Professional		Managerial, Entrepreneurial		Clerical, Sales, White Collar		Skilled, Semi-Skilled, Blue Collar		Housewife		Retired		Student	
	Number of Respondents	Per-cent	Number of Respondents	Per-cent	Number of Respondents	Per-cent	Number of Respondents	Per-cent	Number of Respondents	Per-cent	Number of Respondents	Per-cent	Number of Respondents	Per-cent
FB PRE 2	—	—	2	1.8	1	0.9	1	0.9	5	4.5	5	4.5	—	—
FB POS 2	7	6.3	1	0.9	2	1.8	5	4.5	2	1.8	—	—	3	2.7
2 GEN AB	7	6.3	2	1.8	8	7.2	8	7.2	16	14.4	1	0.9	1	0.9
3 GEN AB	6	5.4	—	—	2	1.8	—	—	3	2.7	—	—	12	10.8
4 GEN AB	3	2.7	—	—	1	0.9	2	1.8	—	—	—	—	5	4.5
ALL FOR	7	6.3	3	2.7	3	2.7	6	5.4	7	6.3	5	4.5	3	2.7
ALL AME	16	14.4	2	1.8	11	9.9	10	9.0	19	17.1	1	0.9	18	16.2
TOTAL	23	20.7	5	4.5	14	12.6	16	14.4	26	23.4	6	5.4	21	18.9

Note: There were no respondents in the Unskilled Blue Collar or Unemployed categories.

Source: Compiled by the author.

88

NEIL C. SANDBERG has been a practitioner in the field of human relations for more than twenty years, lecturing and writing extensively on ethnic, cultural, and intergroup problems in a plural society. As Western Regional Director of the American Jewish Committee, he is an adviser on community relations to a number of government, private, and religious institutions.

Dr. Sandberg is Professor of Sociology and Director of the Institute for Intergroup Relations Training at Loyola Marymount University in Los Angeles. He holds a B.A. from Columbia University and an M.Pl. and Ph.D. from the University of Southern California. He is co-editor with UCLA Dean Harvey S. Perloff of *New Towns: Why—and for Whom?*, published by Praeger in 1973.

Dr. Sandberg is a consultant to the City of Los Angeles on problems of urban development. Recently he served as Chairman of the California Service Alliance, a committee convened by the Governor to coordinate the programs of voluntary organizations. He was also a member of the Attorney General's Commission studying police-community relations in California.

ETHNIC AND RACIAL SEGREGATION IN THE NEW YORK
METROPOLIS:
Residential Patterns Among White Ethnic Groups, Blacks, and Puε
Ricans

Nathan Kantrowitz

THE WHITE ETHNIC MOVEMENT AND ETHNIC POLITICS

Perry L. Weed

RACE MIXING IN THE PUBLIC SCHOOLS

Charles V. Willie
with Jerome Beker

BLACK STUDENTS AT WHITE COLLEGES

Charles V. Willie and
Arlene Sakuma McCord